A GUIDE TO QU.
META-SYNTHESI

A Guide to Qualitative Meta-synthesis provides accessible guidelines for conducting all phases of theory-generating meta-synthesis research, including data collection, analysis, and theory generation. It is a research methodology that is designed to generate evidence-based theory by extracting, analyzing, and synthesizing qualitative findings from across published investigations. These theories provide scaffolding that can be used by health-care providers and other professionals to make context-based decisions and implement situation-specific actions.

Theory-generating meta-synthesis methods stem from the qualitative research paradigm, especially grounded theory. Systematic and rigorous methods are used to identify topically related research reports that provide qualitative findings for analysis. The subsequent analysis of the data goes beyond merely reorganizing and recategorizing research findings. Newly synthesized concepts are developed, and the dynamic relationships among them are fully articulated. The validity of the resultant theory is ensured based on theoretical, methodological, and researcher triangulation; unbiased data collection and sampling strategies; inductive-deductive data analysis and synthesis strategies; and continuous reflexivity.

Meta-synthesis-generated theories are highly important in environments where the use of normalized algorithms, guidelines, and protocols are on the rise. The types of theories discussed in this book will help service providers customize standardized tools so that the most effective evidence-based, yet individualized, interventions can be implemented.

Deborah Finfgeld-Connett, PhD, RN, FAAN, is Professor Emerita of the Sinclair School of Nursing, University of Missouri, Columbia, Missouri, USA. Dr. Finfgeld-Connett has been conducting health-care-related qualitative meta-synthesis research since the mid-1990s. During that time, she has worked to develop and fine-tune the methods that are presented in this textbook.

A GUIDE TO QUALITATIVE META-SYNTHESIS

Deborah Finfgeld-Connett

Routledge
Taylor & Francis Group

NEW YORK AND LONDON

First published 2018
by Routledge
711 Third Avenue, New York, NY 10017

and by Routledge
2 Park Square, Milton Park, Abingdon, Oxon, OX14 4RN

Routledge is an imprint of the Taylor & Francis Group, an informa business

Library of Congress Cataloging-in-Publication Data
Names: Finfgeld-Connett, Deborah, author.
Title: A guide to qualitative meta-synthesis / Deborah Finfgeld-Connett.
Description: New York, NY : Routledge, 2018. | Includes
  bibliographical references.
Identifiers: LCCN 2017052382 | ISBN 9780815380597 (hbk) |
  ISBN 9780815380627 (pbk) | ISBN 9781351212793 (ebk)
Subjects: LCSH: Meta-analysis. | Medicine—Research—Evaluation.
Classification: LCC R853.M48 F56 2018 | DDC 610.72/1—dc23
LC record available at https://lccn.loc.gov/2017052382

ISBN: 978-0-8153-8059-7 (hbk)
ISBN: 978-0-8153-8062-7 (pbk)
ISBN: 978-1-3512-1279-3 (ebk)

Typeset in Bembo
by Apex CoVantage, LLC

CONTENTS

PREFACE

Theories have been generated using primary qualitative research methods (e.g., grounded theory [Corbin & Strauss, 2008]) for many years; however, these theories are generally not considered to be transferable outside of the context in which they were developed. This is because they stem from highly circumscribed samples. The meta-synthesis methods that are described in this text were developed to overcome this barrier and to make qualitative research findings more generalizable. Using the explicated methods, qualitative findings from across primary investigations can be synthesized to develop generalizable, yet context-rich, theory.

Development of generalizable context-rich theory is highly important because practice disciplines increasingly use standardized algorithms, protocols, and guidelines; and theory is needed to contextualize and individualize these prescriptive aids. For instance, given a context-rich meta-synthesis-generated theory, practice guidelines can be adapted to accommodate factors relating to culture, age, and gender; social, psychological, and developmental attributes; spiritual preferences; environmental contingencies; and so forth. Without this type of theoretical backdrop, service providers are at risk of acting in inefficient or ineffective ways.

This handbook is intended for students and scholars who have a basic understanding of qualitative research methods. Although it was written from a healthcare perspective, the methodological principles that are discussed are applicable to professionals from other disciplines such as education and social work.

This text is organized so that researchers can easily read from the beginning to the end in a short period of time. Thereafter, each chapter can be independently studied to enhance understanding. The chapters follow the research process, and they are entitled: (1) *Introduction to Theory-Generating Meta-synthesis Research*; (2) *Research Purpose, Topic, Questions, and Hypotheses*; (3) *Data Collection and*

Sampling; (4) *Data Extraction, Analysis, and Theory Generation;* and (5) *Writing Up the Results.* The sixth and final chapter is entitled *Looking Ahead,* and it includes insights relating to how meta-synthesis-generated theory can be used and updated. Optional learning activities are located at the end of each chapter to help readers understand and immediately engage in the research process.

Although most of the terminology that is used throughout this handbook should be familiar to readers who have a basic understanding of qualitative methods, terms that are particularly significant to theory-generating meta-synthesis research are listed in a glossary near the end of the handbook. In addition, a list of theory-generating meta-synthesis research reports can be found in Appendix 1, and to help researchers easily grasp the entirety of the research process, three theory-generating meta-synthesis articles can be found in Appendices 2, 3, and 4.

Deborah Finfgeld-Connett

References

Corbin, J., & Strauss, A. (2008). *Basics of qualitative research 3e: Techniques and procedures for developing grounded theory.* Thousand Oaks, CA: Sage.

ACKNOWLEDGEMENT

I gratefully acknowledge Dr. Janice Morse, who encouraged me to write this text and who offered valuable feedback along the way.

1

INTRODUCTION TO THEORY-GENERATING META-SYNTHESIS RESEARCH

Deborah Finfgeld-Connett

Theory-generating meta-synthesis research is discussed in this chapter, including how it differs from primary qualitative research and other types of meta-synthesis investigations. The research method is briefly described along with ways in which resultant theories can be used to guide individualized patient care.

Meta-synthesis-generated Theories

Theories offer frameworks for understanding the world in which we live, and they range from being very abstract (e.g., systems theories) to being quite specific (e.g., pharmacodynamics of insulin therapy). Meta-synthesis-generated theories fall in the middle of this vast continuum. As such, they are broad enough to be generalizable and yet focused enough to be contextually relevant. Due to both their generalizability and their contextual relevancy, they have the potential to guide decision-making and action in real-world situations (e.g., see the theory of intimate partner violence and its resolution among Native Americans ([Finfgeld-Connett, 2015] in Appendix 3).

Meta-synthesis-generated theories explicate processes, which are comprised of concepts and the dynamic relationships among them. Concepts (e.g., intimate partner violence [IPV] among Native Americans) and their dynamic relationships (e.g., the relationship between the erosion of Native American culture and the incidence of IPV) are well defined phenomena that are developed by analyzing and synthesizing qualitative research findings from across a representative sample of topically relevant research reports (Finfgeld-Connett, 2015).

Background of Meta-synthesis Research

Many quantitative and qualitative systematic review methods have been developed to maximize the understanding and use of findings from primary research, and scholars are struggling to clearly define and differentiate them. As of 2009, Grant and Booth identified 14 such methods, which vary in terms of purpose and the types of evidence that are analyzed (e.g., qualitative findings, quantitative findings, or both). Since 2009, several qualitative synthesis methods have been refined; however, questions remain regarding how these investigations should be conducted (Tricco et al., 2016). This is due in part to the fact that methods from across multiple qualitative synthesis methodologies are often amalgamated to conduct a single investigation (Paterson, 2012). To diminish this confusion, the purpose of this handbook is to explicate a methodology for synthesizing findings from across primary qualitative research reports to generate theory.

Since the early 1980s, when contemporary qualitative research methods were formalized, countless primary qualitative research investigations have been conducted. Although findings from these investigations have enhanced our knowledge of contextually specific phenomena and processes, these isolated findings have had limited impact on practice (Finfgeld-Connett, 2010). In the late 1980s, qualitative researchers recognized this problem, and the first meta-synthesis methods were developed to synthesize isolated qualitative research findings across studies to make them more meaningful and generalizable (e.g., Noblit & Hare, 1988). Currently, the need to rigorously synthesize qualitative research findings is growing, because the number of primary qualitative investigations is proliferating, and there is an increased demand for contextually rich generalizable findings to help guide evidence-based practice (Finfgeld-Connett, 2010).

Overview of Several Types of Meta-syntheses

Several methods for conducting meta-syntheses exist, which are referred to as meta-ethnography, meta-study, meta-summary, qualitative research synthesis, qualitative meta-aggregation, and so forth (see Table 1.1). Meta-ethnography was developed first, and the purpose of this approach is to synthesize qualitative findings across investigations to create new holistic interpretations (Noblit & Hare, 1988). The purpose of meta-study methods is to analyze theories, methods, and findings across primary qualitative investigations (Paterson, Thorne, Canam, & Jillings, 2001), whereas, the thrust of qualitative research synthesis is to generate conceptual translations across qualitative investigations (Major & Savin-Baden, 2010). Finally, the aim of qualitative meta-aggregation and meta-summary is to sum up and distill information to draw conclusions (Joanna Briggs Institute, 2014; Sandelowski & Barroso, 2007).

Two other methods for synthesizing qualitative research findings are available; however, raw data are not limited to qualitative findings. Realist reviews include quantitative research findings and conceptual and critical literature (Pawson, 2006), and critical interpretive syntheses incorporate quantitative research findings

TABLE 1.1 Methods for Synthesizing Isolated Qualitative Findings: Distinguishing Attributes and Examples

Method	Purpose	Sample	Quality Appraisal	Data Analysis	Examples
Meta-ethnography (Noblit & Hare, 1988)	Synthesize qualitative findings across investigations to create new holistic interpretations	Topically related ethnographic research reports	Appraisal of raw data during analysis	Unspecified, usually some form of thematic analysis	Topic: Mothering children in homeless shelters Purpose: Synthesize qualitative literature relating to homeless women who are mothering children while living in a shelter N = 18 Findings: Six themes—becoming homeless, protective mothering, loss, stressed and depressed, survival strategies, and strategies for resolution (Meadows–Oliver, 2003)
Meta-study (Paterson et al., 2001)	Analyze theories, methods, and findings across primary qualitative investigations	Representative sample of primary qualitative research reports	Appraisal of reports based on consensus of research team	Coding, categorizing	Topic: Perception of chronic illness over time N = 292 Findings: Chronic illness is perceived to involve a continuous process of managing perceptions of illness versus wellness (Paterson, 2001).
Qualitative research synthesis (Major & Savin–Baden, 2010)	Develop a conceptual translation, a reinterpretation or a new theory	Purposeful sampling of primary qualitative research reports to reach saturation	Appraisal of reports based on listed criteria	Thematic analysis	Topic: Faculty experiences of teaching online N = 9 Findings: Online teaching changes the way faculty approach and think about teaching, course design, time, instruction, and students (Major, 2010).

(Continued)

TABLE 1.1 (Continued)

Method	Purpose	Sample	Quality Appraisal	Data Analysis	Examples
Meta-summary (Sandelowski & Barroso, 2007)	Sum up (i.e., aggregate) and synthesize knowledge to draw conclusions	Exhaustive search of qualitative research reports	Appraisal of reports based on listed criteria	Aggregation and distillation of findings from primary studies	Topic: Stigma among HIV-positive women N = 93 Findings: HIV-positive women perceive that stigma is pervasive and intense. Management of stigma involves efforts to control information to preserve interpersonal relationships and to maintain moral identity (Sandelowski, Lambe, & Barroso, 2004).
Meta-aggregation (Joanna Briggs Institute [JBI], 2014)	Create cross-case generalizations	Exhaustive search of qualitative research reports	Appraisal of reports base on JBI instrument	Aggregation and distillation of findings using JBI computer software	Topic: Young peoples' experience of chronic illness N = 18 Findings: Chronic illness makes young people feel uncomfortable, disrupts normal life, and is not all bad. There are ways to minimize mental health problems and get through the experience (Venning, Eliott, Wilson, & Kettler, 2006).
Realist review (Pawson, 2006)	Test and refine program theory	Qualitative and quantitative research reports plus conceptual and critical literature	Appraisal of raw data during analysis	Emergent, depends on data	Topic: Effective and preferred intermediate care at home N = 193 Findings: To achieve the goals of intermediate care, it is important to involve service users and their care providers in collaborative decision-making (Pearson et al., 2015).

Critical interpretive synthesis (Dixon-Woods et al., 2006)	Critique, generate themes, and produce a new theoretical conceptualization	Qualitative and quantitative research reports plus reviews	Appraisal emergent and varies depending on type of report/findings	Emergent, depends on data	Topic: Conceptualize cancer information provision N = 57 Findings: The process of cancer information provision recognizes the diverse, changing, and relational nature of patients' values, needs, and preferences. It accommodates various levels of patient involvement, and it ensures timely provision of selected and personally relevant information (Kazimierczak et al., 2013).
Cochrane (Noyes et al., 2015)	Enhance, extend, or supplement results of meta-analyses	Qualitative research reports that enhance Cochrane meta-analysis findings	Appraisal of reports based on established instrument	Emergent, depends on nature of investigation	Topic: Engagement of maternal–child lay health workers N = 53 Findings: Factors that influence the engagement of maternal–child lay health workers include close relationships between workers and recipients; services that recipients perceive as relevant; regular and visible support from the health system and the community; and appropriate training, supervision, and incentives (Glenton et al., 2013).
Theory-generating meta-synthesis (Finfgeld-Connett, 2014a, 2014b; Finfgeld-Connett & Johnson, 2013)	Generate theory across primary qualitative investigations	Theoretical sampling of primary qualitative research reports to reach saturation	Appraisal of raw data during analysis	Coding, categorizing, memoing, diagramming	Topic: Intimate partner violence (IPV) among Native Americans N = 13 Findings: Theory of IPV and its resolution among Native Americans (Finfgeld-Connett, 2015)

(Dixon-Woods et al., 2006). Given the variety of research questions and the raw data that are involved in these types of investigations, the data analysis methods tend to be emergent and somewhat unique to each study.

An underlying assumption of the meta-syntheses discussed so far is that they are comprehensive standalone studies. This contrasts with qualitative syntheses that are primarily intended to be adjuncts or extensions of quantitative meta-analyses. In these instances, findings from across quantitative studies are analyzed to identify statistically significant results (Polit & Beck, 2017), and findings from qualitative syntheses are used to texturize them (e.g., Cochrane [Noyes et al., 2015]).

The meta-synthesis methodology that is outlined in this handbook is meant to result in findings that are fully meaningful on their own. Unlike other approaches, however, the primary objective of this approach is to generate theory. Consistent with this goal, the methods outlined in this text are based on grounded theory, which is an inductive research methodology that involves theoretical sampling, rigorous data analysis and synthesis, and the development of a process model (Corbin & Strauss, 2008). Process models are particularly important to health-care practitioners because step-by-step assessment, action, and reassessment are fundamental to enhancing the mental and physical well-being of patients.

Methodological Labeling

Prior to focusing on theory-generating meta-synthesis, methodological labeling needs to be briefly addressed. As suggested in column 1 of Table 1.1, confusion abounds (Britten, Garside, Pope, Frost, & Cooper, 2017; Thorne, 2017); and the body of work relating to theory-generating meta-synthesis is no exception. Over time, researchers have used terms such as meta-synthesis, meta-interpretation, and qualitative systematic review. This inconsistency is regrettable; however, it reflects the emergent nature of the research genre. It also reflects progressive efforts to label research methods so that readers and reviewers will understand them and support their use (Cheek, 2017). With a few exceptions (e.g., Appendices 2, 3, and 4), the term that is used in the remainder of this text is theory-generating meta-synthesis. For purposes of readability, it is occasionally shortened to meta-synthesis.

Overview of Theory-Generating Meta-synthesis Research Process

Theory-generating meta-synthesis research is positioned within the qualitative research paradigm, and it is based on grounded theory methods (Corbin & Strauss, 2008). In keeping with this paradigmatic and methodological orientation, theory-generating meta-synthesis research is founded on the assumption that theory can be inductively generated from qualitative data. In this case, data consist of qualitative findings that have been extracted from published research reports. The research process is iterative, and theory emerges as data analysis and synthesis progress over time (Finfgeld-Connett, 2010, 2014b).

Theory-generating meta-synthesis investigations are conducted by analyzing and synthesizing published qualitative research findings (i.e., raw data) from across multiple primary qualitative or multi-method studies. Results go beyond the aggregation and summation of existing findings to constitute newly synthesized theory that has the potential to underpin decision-making and action (Finfgeld-Connett, 2010).

Comparison of Theory-Generating Meta-synthesis Methods and Primary Qualitative Research

In addition to understanding the similarities and differences among meta-synthesis research methods, it is also important to understand the similarities and differences between primary qualitative research and theory-generating meta-synthesis (see Table 1.2).

TABLE 1.2 Comparison of Primary Qualitative Research and Theory-Generating Meta-synthesis Research

Elements of Research	Primary Qualitative Research	Theory-Generating Meta-synthesis Research
Research Theoretical Framework	Grounded theory, phenomenology, ethnography, etc.	Grounded theory
Purpose	Describe, explore, or understand phenomena or generate theory with limited generalizability beyond the study sample	Generate process theory that is generalizable (i.e., transferable) beyond the study sample
Research Questions	Relate to describing, exploring, or understanding phenomena/concepts	Relate to explicating antecedents, attributes, and outcomes of process theory
Hypotheses	Continually developed and adapted throughout data collection and analysis	Continually developed and adapted throughout data collection and analysis
Data Collection and Sampling	Theoretical or purposeful collection of data via individual interviews, focus groups, diaries, etc.	Theoretical assemblage of published research reports and extraction of qualitative research findings
Raw Data	Typically, text-based data that are extracted from interviews, focus groups, diaries, etc.	Qualitative research findings that are extracted from published research reports
Data Analysis Methods	Thematic or content analysis of raw data to answer research questions	Content analysis and synthesis of published research findings to explicate concepts and the dynamic relationships among them
Findings	Descriptions, themes, concepts, and frameworks with limited generalizability	Process frameworks (i.e., theories) that are generalizable (i.e., transferable) beyond the study sample

Whereas theory-generating meta-synthesis research is based on grounded theory (Corbin & Strauss, 2008), primary qualitative research can be underpinned by grounded theory as well as other research theoretical frameworks such as phenomenology and ethnography. The purpose of primary qualitative research is to describe, explore, or understand phenomena, as well as to generate contextually specific theory. Conversely, theory-generating meta-syntheses are intended to result in newly synthesized theories that are transferable (i.e., generalizable) beyond the samples from which they originated. Generalizability of findings from theory-generating meta-syntheses is possible because the research investigations that make up the sample are not replication studies. Thus, heterogeneity within the study sample broadens the applicability of the findings (Finfgeld-Connett, 2010).

Research questions that drive primary qualitative research largely focus on describing, exploring, or understanding phenomena/concepts; whereas, those relating to theory-generating meta-syntheses pertain to explicating antecedents, attributes, and outcomes of processes. In both instances, research questions and tentative hypotheses are continually posed throughout data collection and analysis (Finfgeld-Connett, 2014a; Polit & Beck, 2017).

When conducting primary qualitative research, data collection can be purposeful or theoretical, and raw data generally consist of text-based data that are gathered from interviews, focus groups, diaries, and so forth. Conversely, when carrying out theory-generating meta-syntheses, theoretical sampling is conducted, and the unit of analysis is fully analyzed qualitative research findings that are extracted from published research reports (Finfgeld-Connett, 2014b; Polit & Beck, 2017).

Thematic or content analysis is largely used to analyze raw data when conducting primary qualitative research. When conducting theory-generating meta-synthesis research, however, data analysis must push beyond mere coding and categorizing. In these instances, data analysis must also involve explicating relationships among concepts to generate process frameworks. The latter is accomplished through memoing and diagramming (Finfgeld-Connett, 2014a, 2014b; Polit & Beck, 2017).

Use of Meta-synthesis-generated Theory in Health Care

Broadly speaking, two types of theories guide clinical practice. The first type is highly generalizable, and it is substantiated by findings from randomized-controlled trials and quantitative meta-analyses. These types of theories result in empirically based patient-care protocols that are essential for delivering high-quality health care (Thorne & Sawatzky, 2014). That said, the proliferation of these types of guidelines is somewhat concerning (Knisely & Draucker, 2016) because they are designed for use across populations rather than in more circumscribed situations (Engebretsen, Vollestad, Wahl, Robinson, & Heggen, 2015; Ou, Hall, & Thorne, 2017; Tanenbaum, 2014).

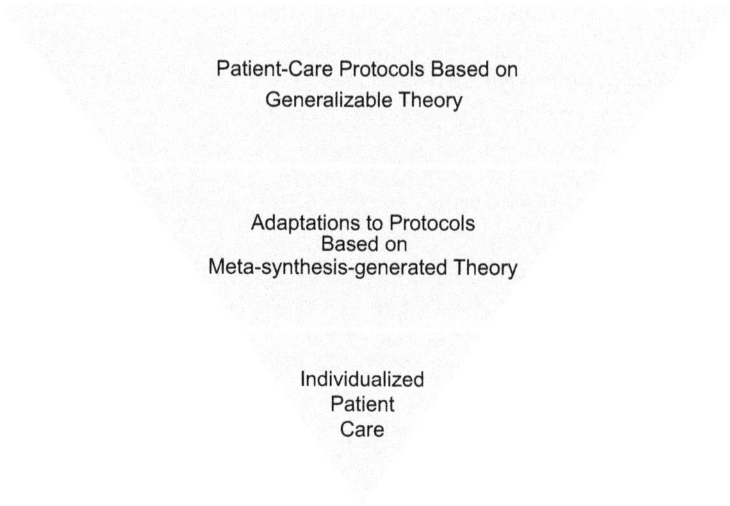

Patient-Care Protocols Based on
Generalizable Theory

Adaptations to Protocols
Based on
Meta-synthesis-generated Theory

Individualized
Patient
Care

FIGURE 1.1 Individualized Patient Care Based on Meta-synthesis-generated Theory

Factors such as ethnicity, race, education, socioeconomic status, and geographic location account for a vast number of health-care contingencies. In addition, unique individual and situational factors result in endless variations within practice (Carlsen, Glenton, & Pope, 2007; Knisely & Draucker, 2016; Polkinghorne, 2004). Failure to customize standardized patient-care guidelines to accommodate these point-of-care differences can result in inefficient or ineffective interventions (Engebretsen et al., 2015; Knisely & Draucker, 2016; Thorne & Sawatzky, 2014).

Meta-synthesis-generated theories consist of well-articulated concepts in dynamic relationships that are explicated in the form of process models. They are generalizable, but at the same time, they are focused and flexible. Meta-synthesis-generated theories provide empirically based storylines (i.e., narratives) for decision-making (Finfgeld-Connett, 2010, 2014a), and they offer insight into temporal and causal events; including their antecedents, attributes, and outcomes. Due to their process structure, meta-synthesis-generated theories make potential intervention points easy to identify; and due to their flexibility, individual patient needs can be accommodated (see Figure 1.1) (Finfgeld-Connett, 2016). The purpose of conducting theory-generating meta-synthesis research will be discussed in greater detail in Chapter 2.

Learning Activities

1. Explain how theory-generating meta-synthesis research differs from primary qualitative research, other types of meta-synthesis research, and quantitative meta-analyses.

2. Discuss how grounded theory underpins theory-generating meta-synthesis research.

3. Discuss how a meta-synthesis-generated theory can be used to individualize evidence-based patient-care protocols/guidelines.

References

Britten, N., Garside, R., Pope, C., Frost, J., & Cooper, C. (2017). Asking more of qualitative synthesis: A response to Sally Thorne. *Qualitative Health Research*. Advance online publication. doi: 10.1177/1049732317709010

Carlsen, B., Glenton, C., & Pope, C. (2007). Thou shalt versus thou shalt not: A meta-synthesis of GPs' attitudes to clinical practice guidelines. *British Journal of General Practice*, *57*, 971–978. doi: 10.3399/096016407782604820

Cheek, J. (2017). Qualitative inquiry and the research marketplace: Putting some +s (pluses) in our thinking, and why this matters. *Cultural Studies ↔ Critical Methodologies*, *17*, 221–226. doi: 10.1177/1532708616669528

Corbin, J., & Strauss, A. (2008). *Basics of qualitative research 3e: Techniques and procedures for developing grounded theory*. Thousand Oaks, CA: Sage.

Dixon-Woods, M., Cavers, D., Agarwal, S., Annandale, E., Arthur, A., Harvey, J., . . . Sutton, A. J. (2006). Conducting a critical interpretive synthesis of the literature on access to healthcare by vulnerable groups. *BMC Medical Research Methodology*, *6*, 35. doi: 10.1186/1471-2288-6-35

Engebretsen, E., Vollestad, N. K., Wahl, A. K., Robinson, H. S., & Heggen, K. (2015). Unpacking the process of interpretation in evidence-based decision making. *Journal of Evaluation in Clinical Practice*, *21*, 529–531. doi: 10.1111/jep.12362

Finfgeld-Connett, D. (2010). Generalizability and transferability of meta-synthesis research findings. *Journal of Advanced Nursing*, *66*, 246–254. doi: 10.1111/j.1365-2648.2009.05250.x

Finfgeld-Connett, D. (2014a). Meta-synthesis findings: Potential versus reality. *Qualitative Health Research*, *24*, 1581–1591. doi: 10.1177/1049732314548878

Finfgeld-Connett, D. (2014b). Use of content analysis to conduct knowledge-building and theory-generating qualitative systematic reviews. *Qualitative Research*, *14*, 341–352. doi: 10.1177/1468794113481790

Finfgeld-Connett, D. (2015). Qualitative systematic review of intimate partner violence among Native Americans. *Issues in Mental Health Nursing*, *36*, 754–760. doi: 10.3109/01612840.2015.1047072

Finfgeld-Connett, D. (2016, May). *Use of meta-synthesis research to generate theory for practice*. Paper presented at 12th Annual Congress of Qualitative Inquiry, Champaign, IL.

Finfgeld-Connett, D., & Johnson, E. D. (2013). Abused South Asian women in Westernized countries and their experiences seeking help. *Issues in Mental Health Nursing*, *34*, 863–873. doi: 10.3109/01612840.2013.833318

Glenton, C., Colvin, C., Carlsen, B., Swartz, A., Lewin, S., Noyes, J., & Rashidian, A. (2013). Barriers and facilitators to the implementation of lay health worker programs to improve access to maternal and child health: Qualitative evidence synthesis. *Cochrane Database of Systematic Reviews* Issue 10. Art. No.: CD010414. Retrieved from http://onlinelibrary.wiley.com/doi/10.1002/14651858.CD010414.pub2/pdf

Grant, M. J., & Booth, A. (2009). A typology of reviews: An analysis of 14 review types and associated methodologies. *Health Information & Libraries Journal, 26*, 91–108. doi: 10.1111/j.1471–1842.2009.00848.x

Joanna Briggs Institute. (2014). *Joanna Briggs Institute reviewers' manual.* Retrieved from www.joannabriggs.org/assets/docs/sumari/ReviewersManual-2014.pdf

Kazimierczak, K. A., Skea, Z. C., Dixon-Woods, M., Entwistle, V. A., Feldman-Stewart, D., N'Dow, J. M., & MacLennan, S. J. (2013). Provision of cancer information as a "support for navigating the knowledge landscape": Findings from a critical interpretive literature synthesis. *European Journal of Oncology Nursing, 17*, 360–369. doi: 10.1016/j.ejon.2012.10.002

Knisely, M. R., & Draucker, C. B. (2016). Using a person-oriented approach in nursing research. *Western Journal of Nursing Research, 38*, 508–520. doi: 10.1177/0193945915602856

Major, C. H. (2010). Do virtual professors dream of electric students? University faculty experiences with online distance education. *Teachers College Record, 112*, 2154–2208.

Major, C. H., & Savin-Baden, M. (2010). *An introduction to qualitative research synthesis: Managing the information explosion in social science research.* New York, NY: Routledge.

Meadows-Oliver, M. (2003). Mothering in public: A meta-synthesis of homeless women with children living in shelters. *Journal for Specialists in Pediatric Nursing, 8*, 130–136. doi: 10.1111/j.1088-145X.2003.00130.x/full

Noblit, G. W., & Hare, R. D. (1988). *Meta-ethnography: Synthesizing qualitative studies.* Newbury Park, CA: Sage.

Noyes, J., Hannes, K., Booth, A., Harris, J., Harden, A., Popay, J., . . . Pantoja, T. (2015). Chapter 20: Qualitative research and Cochrane reviews: Supplemental handbook guidance. In J. P. T. Higgins & S. Green (Eds.), *Cochrane handbook for systematic reviews of interventions.* Version 5.3.0. The Cochrane Collaboration. Retrieved from http://qim.cochrane.org/supplemental-handbook-guidance

Ou, C. H. K., Hall, W. A., & Thorne, S. E. (2017). Can nursing epistemology embrace *p*-values? *Nursing Philosophy.* Advance online publication. doi: 10.1111/nup.12173

Paterson, B. L. (2001). The shifting perspectives model of chronic illness. *Journal of Nursing Scholarship, 33*, 21–26. doi: 10.1111/j.1547-5069.2001.00021.x

Paterson, B. L. (2012). "It looks great but how do I know if it fits?" An introduction to meta-synthesis research. In K. Hannes & C. Lockwood (Eds.), *Synthesizing qualitative research: Choosing the right approach* (pp. 1–20). Oxford, UK: Wiley-Blackwell.

Paterson, B. L., Thorne, S. E., Canam, C., & Jillings, C. (2001). *Meta-study of qualitative health research: A practical guide to meta-analysis and meta-synthesis.* Thousand Oaks, CA: Sage.

Pawson, R. (2006). *Evidence-based policy: A realist perspective.* Los Angeles: Sage.

Pearson, M., Hunt, H., Cooper, C., Shepperd, S., Pawson, R., & Anderson, R. (2015). Providing effective and preferred care closer to home: A realist review of intermediate care. *Health & Social Care in the Community, 23*, 577–593. doi: 10.1111/hsc.12183

Polit, D. F., & Beck, C. T. (2017). *Nursing research: Generating and assessing evidence for nursing practice* (10th ed.). Philadelphia: Wolters Kluwer.

Polkinghorne, D. E. (2004). *Practice and the human sciences: The case for judgment-based patient care.* Albany: State University of New York.

Sandelowski, M., & Barroso, J. (2007). *Handbook for synthesizing qualitative research.* New York, NY: Springer.

Sandelowski, M., Lambe, C., & Barroso, J. (2004). Stigma in HIV-positive women. *Journal of Nursing Scholarship, 36*, 122–128. doi: 10.1111/j.1547-5069.2004.04024.x

Tanenbaum, S. J. (2014). Particularism in health care: Challenging the authority of the aggregate. *Journal of Evaluation in Clinical Practice, 20*, 934–941. doi: 10.1111/jep.12249

Thorne, S. (2017). Advancing the field of synthesis scholarship: A response to Nicky Britten and colleagues. *Qualitative Health Research.* Advance online publication. doi: 10.1177/1049732317711190

Thorne, S., & Sawatzky, R. (2014). Particularizing the general: Sustaining theoretical integrity in the context of an evidence-based practice agenda. *Advances in Nursing Science, 37*, 5–18. doi: 10.1097/ANS.0000000000000011

Tricco, A. C., Soobiah, C., Antony, J., Cogo, E., MacDonald, H., Lillie, E., . . . Kastner, M. (2016). A scoping review identifies multiple emerging knowledge synthesis methods, but few studies operationalize the method. *Journal of Clinical Epidemiology, 73*, 19–28. doi: 10.1016/j.jclinepi.2015.08.030

Venning, A., Eliott, J., Wilson, A., & Kettler, L. (2006). Understanding young peoples' experience of chronic illness: A systematic review. *JBI Library of Systematic Reviews, 4*, 1–40. doi: 10.11124/jbisrir-2006-753

2

RESEARCH PURPOSE, TOPIC, QUESTIONS, AND HYPOTHESES

Deborah Finfgeld-Connett

The purpose of conducting theory-generating meta-synthesis research is discussed in this chapter. In addition, topic statements, questions, and hypotheses that are consistent with theory-generating meta-synthesis research are examined.

Purpose of Theory-Generating Meta-synthesis Research

Commonalities exist across every human experience; however, a single lens is not appropriate for interpreting every situation. To bring human experiences into focus, contextualization is necessary, and meta-synthesis-generated theories help to do this. In effect, they make situational circumstances clearer and more meaningful so that decisions and actions can be more context specific.

The meta-synthesis methods that are outlined in this handbook can be used to extend, adapt, or develop new theories. With this in mind, the general purpose of theory-generating meta-synthesis research is to explicate well-delineated concepts in relationship. This contrasts with many primary qualitative research investigations and meta-syntheses wherein the main purpose is to aggregate data or to explore and explicate concepts or phenomena without necessarily articulating the dynamic relationships among them (Finfgeld-Connett, 2014b).

Consistent with concepts in dynamic relationship is change over time, or simply stated, process. Elements of process include phenomena and their antecedents and outcomes. Although these elements might not be overtly obvious in all theory-generating meta-synthesis purpose statements, they comprise the underlying foundation (Finfgeld-Connett, 2014b). Examples of meta-synthesis purpose statements that are written as process statements are listed below.

1. Explicate the process of managing life in the context of early-stage dementia.
2. Understand how end-of-life care can be optimized for patients who choose to remain in their homes.

3. Delineate the process involved in successfully introducing innovative care procedures in long-term care facilities.
4. Articulate how knowledge about seasonal flu transmission affects prevention efforts.

Topics

Origins

Topics for meta-synthesis investigations are commonly generated in two ways. First, qualitative researchers recognize that by synthesizing findings from their own topically related investigations, and potentially those of others, they can generate more informative findings (Finfgeld, 2003). This was the case with a series of qualitative investigations relating to courage and the management of long-term health concerns. In this instance, findings from several primary qualitative research investigations were synthesized, and a more complete and generalizable theory of becoming and being courageous in the midst of enduring health problems was developed (Finfgeld, 1999). The same potential was recognized in relationship to a series of primary qualitative investigations that focused on self-resolution of drug and alcohol problems, and a more informative and transferable framework was generated (Finfgeld, 2000).

Theory-generating meta-synthesis topics are also identified when investigators have not conducted primary qualitative research in a specific area, but they are aware that findings from several topically related primary qualitative investigations are available. In these instances, researchers hypothesize that theory development is possible based on the synthesis of findings from across investigations. This was the case when a theory-generating meta-synthesis was carried out to examine the process of transitioning from being a non-bachelor's prepared registered nurse to a registered nurse with a bachelor's degree (Anbari, 2015). It was also the case in relationship to a theory-generating meta-synthesis that pertained to the process of interviewing victims of intimate partner violence (Snyder, 2016).

Topic Development

Consistent with the qualitative research paradigm, meta-synthesis research topics are context specific. At the same time, the goal of theory-generating meta-synthesis research is to produce findings that are generalizable. As such, theory-generating meta-synthesis topics should be contextually relevant and yet broad enough to yield findings that are transferable beyond the meta-synthesis sample (Finfgeld-Connett, 2010).

For example, when preparing to conduct a theory-generating meta-synthesis relating to intimate partner violence, this expansive topic was judged to be too broad to yield contextually meaningful findings because cultural attributes of specific groups could not be adequately considered. Thus, the topic was reframed based on context-specific subgroups (e.g., older women [Finfgeld-Connett, 2014a];

African American, Native American, and Mexican immigrant women [Finfgeld-Connett, 2015a, 2015b, 2017]; South Asian immigrant women [Finfgeld-Connett & Johnson, 2013]), and separate meta-syntheses were conducted. The resultant findings from each of these meta-syntheses were both contextually specific and transferable to the real world.

Although some topics might be too narrow to be generalizable, this problem is apt to be self-correcting because sufficient numbers of research reports to conduct a theory-generating meta-synthesis will be difficult to assemble given a very circumscribed focus. In these situations, researchers are encouraged to consider whether they can broaden a research topic while maintaining the original intent of the investigation. For example, when conducting a meta-synthesis of intimate partner violence among Native Americans, including research reports relating to indigenous people from Canada instead of just the United States resulted in a sample that could support the development of a generalizable theory without jeopardizing the contextual relevancy of the findings (Finfgeld-Connett, 2015b).

Research Questions

From the outset of a theory-generating meta-synthesis investigation, the extent to which a theory can be developed cannot be fully known. Unlike primary qualitative research, wherein the researcher can continue to collect data to develop specific aspects of a theory, meta-synthesis researchers are limited by the number of published investigations that are currently available (Finfgeld, 2003). Thus, at the start of a theory-generating meta-synthesis investigation, broad questions are posed that guide the researcher toward the explication of a process. Initial research questions target general attributes of processes, including antecedents and outcomes. Later, during data analysis, more focused questions are developed to help delineate emergent aspects of the theoretical framework (see Table 2.1).

TABLE 2.1 Theory-Generating Meta-synthesis Research Questions Relating to Mexican American Women (Finfgeld-Connett, 2017)

Initial Research Questions
- What are the antecedents of intimate partner violence?
- How and why is intimate partner violence sustained over time?
- What tends to motivate women to resolve intimate partner violence?
- How can health-care providers optimally assist to resolve intimate partner violence?
- What are the outcomes of resolving intimate partner violence?

Additional Questions (Examples)
- What role does machismo play in the occurrence of intimate partner violence?
- What self-nurturing strategies are used by Mexican American women that paradoxically sustain intimate partner violence?
- How do Mexican American women identify trustworthy service providers?
- How do Mexican American women describe the process of self-transformation that occurs as intimate partner violence is resolved?

Hypotheses

When conducting theory-generating meta-synthesis research, hypothesis develop-ment differs from the way it occurs when carrying out quantitative research. In conjunction with quantitative investigations, hypotheses are posed at the outset, and they remain unchanged throughout the study. At the end of a quantitative inves-tigation, a judgment is made about whether the hypotheses are supported based on the findings (Polit & Beck, 2017). Conversely, when conducting theory-generating meta-syntheses, hypotheses are tentatively posed at the outset of an investigation. Thereafter, they are continually juxtaposed with the data, and inferentially rejected, revised, or supported until data analysis is complete (Finfgeld-Connett, 2014b).

When conducting theory-generating research, ongoing development of hypotheses is particularly helpful in terms of examining process elements. For example, in regard to an investigation relating to older abused women, it was originally hypothesized that health-care providers should be direct and forthright when helping them to escape from abusive partners. As the research progressed, however, it became clear that change was complex, and more specific hypotheses were developed relating to exactly when and how it was practical for health-care providers to therapeutically intervene (Finfgeld-Connett, 2014a). Similarly, while investigating aggression and therapeutic interventions among hospitalized psy-chiatric patients, it was hypothesized that emergent aggression could be managed using normalizing strategies. As data analysis progressed, however, this hypothesis was rejected and replaced by hypotheses relating to the therapeutic use of mutu-ality and limit setting (Finfgeld-Connett, 2009).

Theory-generating meta-synthesis research methods are fluid and iterative. As such, research questions and hypotheses are continually posed as data collection and analysis commence and progress. Data collection will be discussed in Chapter 3 followed by a discussion of data analysis in Chapter 4.

Learning Activities

1. Based on your research interest area, identify a topic that could be investigated using theory-generating meta-synthesis methods.
2. Based on your identified topic, generate a purpose statement, research ques-tions, and tentative hypotheses that could be investigated using theory-generating meta-synthesis methods.

References

Anbari, A. B. (2015). The RN to BSN transition: A qualitative systematic review. *Global Qualitative Nursing Research, 2*, 1–11. Retrieved from http://journals.sagepub.com/doi/pdf/10.1177/2333393615614306

Finfgeld, D. L. (1999). Courage as a process of pushing beyond the struggle. *Qualitative Health Research, 9*, 803–814. doi: 10.1177/104973299129122298

Finfgeld, D. L. (2000). Self-resolution of drug and alcohol problems: A synthesis of qualitative findings. *Journal of Addictions Nursing, 12*, 65–72.

Finfgeld, D. L. (2003). Meta-synthesis: The state of the art—so far. *Qualitative Health Research, 13*, 893–904. doi: 10.1177/1049732303253462

Finfgeld-Connett, D. (2009). Model of therapeutic and non-therapeutic responses to patient aggression. *Issues in Mental Health Nursing, 30*, 530–537. doi: 10.1080/01612840902722120

Finfgeld-Connett, D. (2010). Generalizability and transferability of meta-synthesis research findings. *Journal of Advanced Nursing, 66*, 246–254. doi: 10.1111/j.1365-2648.2009.05250.x

Finfgeld-Connett, D. (2014a). Intimate partner abuse among older women: Qualitative systematic review. *Clinical Nursing Research, 23*, 664–683. doi: 10.1177/1054773813500301

Finfgeld-Connett, D. (2014b). Meta-synthesis findings: Potential versus reality. *Qualitative Health Research, 24*, 1581–1591. doi: 10.1177/1049732314548878

Finfgeld-Connett, D. (2015a). Intimate partner violence and its resolution among African American women. *Global Qualitative Nursing Research, 2*, 1–8. Retrieved from http://journals.sagepub.com/doi/pdf/10.1177/2333393614565182

Finfgeld-Connett, D. (2015b). Qualitative systematic review of intimate partner violence among Native Americans. *Issues in Mental Health Nursing, 36*, 754–760. doi: 10.3109/01612840.2015.1047072

Finfgeld-Connett, D. (2017). Intimate partner violence and its resolution among Mexican Americans. *Issues in Mental Health Nursing, 38*, 464–472. doi: 10.1080/01612840.2017.1284968

Finfgeld-Connett, D., & Johnson, E. D. (2013). Abused South Asian women in western-ized countries and their experiences seeking help. *Issues in Mental Health Nursing, 34*, 863–873. doi: 10.3109/01612840.2013.833318

Polit, D. F., & Beck, C. T. (2017). *Nursing research: Generating and assessing evidence for nursing practice* (10th ed.). Philadelphia, PA: Wolters Kluwer.

Snyder, B. L. (2016). Women's experience of being interviewed about abuse: A qualitative systematic review. *Journal of Psychiatric and Mental Health Nursing, 23*, 605–613. doi: 10.1111/jpm.12353

3

DATA COLLECTION AND SAMPLING

Deborah Finfgeld-Connett and E. Diane Johnson

The aim of data collection and sampling is covered in this chapter. In addition, resources and tools that are necessary for data collection are examined along with the types of research reports that should be included in a theory-generating meta-synthesis investigation. Principles of theoretical searching and sampling are discussed along with efficient and effective strategies for searching the literature.

Aim of Data Collection and Sampling

When conducting theory-generating meta-synthesis research, the aim of data collection is to assemble an unbiased sample of published qualitative or mixed-method research reports that support the full explication of process theory. In general, bias is "any influence that distorts the results of a study and undermines validity" (Polit & Beck, 2017, p. 720). In the case of theory-generating research, an unrepresentative sample is one source of bias. Primary ways to avoid this problem include positioning oneself within an institution that supports a comprehensive state-of-the-art research library, and expansively and skillfully searching across multiple discipline-specific databases for topically relevant research reports. In addition, an unrepresentative sample is avoided by expertly applying theoretical sampling strategies to generate an impartial collection of research reports for analysis. These strategies are discussed throughout this chapter.

Qualitative findings that are extracted from these reports constitute the raw data for analysis. Validity of the emergent theory is based on saturation or fit, which signals the cessation of data collection. Data collection is not guided by the need to exhaustively validate emergent concepts or their relationships beyond the point of saturation or fit. As such, theoretical versus exhaustive data collection is the aim (Finfgeld-Connett & Johnson, 2013).

Theoretical sampling[1] involves an iterative process of searching for and selecting reports for inclusion in the study sample. Sampling is initiated based on preliminary assumptions about the type of research reports that are needed to generate a context-specific theory. Thereafter, searching and sampling strategies are subject to change so that gaps in the emergent theory can be filled and coding categories can be saturated.

Qualitative research findings, which constitute the raw data for theory-generating meta-synthesis investigations, are extracted from published primary research reports that are available in the public domain. Unanalyzed data that are collected from human subjects are not included in the database. Thus, theory-generating meta-synthesis research is not subject to Institutional Review Board approval.

Preliminary Literature Search

It is often unclear from the outset of a theory-generating meta-synthesis investigation what the existing literature will support. Thus, a preliminary search and review of the literature is recommended to determine whether the pool of topically related qualitative research reports is adequate to generate valid theory (Finfgeld, 2003; Finfgeld-Connett & Johnson, 2013). Depending on the extent of this type of preliminary searching, a standalone review of the literature (i.e., scoping review [Arksey & O'Malley, 2005]) could result. When conducting a theory-generating meta-synthesis investigation, however, the primary purpose of this type of review is to simply understand the volume and type of literature that is available for rigorous synthesis.

Resources

Setting

To ensure an adequate sample, theory-generating meta-synthesis investigators are urged to position themselves within a research-intensive university that supports a state-of-the-art academic library. A broad selection of electronic reference databases is necessary along with access to a comprehensive collection of cross-disciplinary research journals.

Research Reports

Research reports that contain qualitative findings and that have been published in peer-reviewed or non-peer-reviewed publications are eligible for inclusion in the sample. Peer-reviewed articles are published in academic journals, and they have undergone a double-blind review process prior to publication. Non-peer-reviewed research reports include government documents, theses, and dissertations. They can also include some scholarly monographs, books, book chapters, and the like. Theoretical and critical literature, field notes, case histories, poems, novels, dramas, stories, and so forth that are not the result of rigorous qualitative research are not eligible for inclusion in the sample (Sandelowski & Barroso, 2003).

Digitized copies of research reports are ideal for meta-synthesis investigations because they can be easily downloaded, stored, and shared among research team members. In addition, electronic copies can be searched and annotated, and raw data (i.e., qualitative research findings) can be extracted for analysis without introducing transcription errors.

Three points should be made about research reports that appear outside of traditional peer-reviewed journals. First, although these types of reports have not been peer-reviewed within the commercial realm, it is likely that they have been vetted by scholars (e.g., faculty, seasoned researchers, etc.) prior to completion. Second, because these reports are not subject to the same page restrictions as articles published in traditional journals, they have the potential to offer in-depth descriptions of methods and rich findings. Third, although there might be fees involved in accessing theses and dissertations, the trend is to make electronic copies available at little or no cost to users through websites such as the Networked Digital Library of Theses and Dissertations (NDLTD at http://search. ndltd.org/) (Finfgeld-Connett & Johnson, 2013; Macduff et al., 2016; Toews et al., 2017).

Reference Databases

In the digital age, literature searching is fundamentally a computer-based activity, and electronic databases (e.g., Cumulative Index to Nursing and Allied Health Literature [CINAHL], PubMed, PsycINFO, Scopus, etc.) are used to systematically search for reports of primary qualitative research. Reference databases can be searched individually or in groups. The latter is accomplished by using search interfaces such as EBSCOhost, which allows for the simultaneous searching of multiple databases such as CINAHL, PsycINFO, MEDLINE, and others (EBSCO Support, n.d.). Apparent advantages of search interfaces aside, meta-synthesis researchers are urged to use them with discretion because the search functions of each database can only be optimized when they are accessed individually.

Databases (e.g., CINAHL, PsycINFO, and MEDLINE) function somewhat differently, and to maximize the potential of each one, specialized knowledge and skills are needed. Fortunately, information and tutorials are readily available online (e.g., CINAHL: http://support.ebsco.com/cinahl/; PubMed: www.nlm. nih.gov/bsd/disted/pubmed.html). In addition, meta-synthesis researchers are encouraged to consult with professional reference librarians, who are experts at searching reference databases. Researchers are also urged to include reference librarians in meta-synthesis grant applications whenever possible.

Three reference databases require special note. The first two are MEDLINE and PubMed, both of which are sometimes searched in conjunction with a single meta-synthesis investigation. Prior to simultaneously searching each one, however, several factors should be considered. First, PubMed includes everything in MED-LINE along with subsets of records that are not fully indexed in MEDLINE. These subsets include in-process records that are being indexed for MEDLINE, journal records that do not meet criteria for MEDLINE indexing, records that are deposited in the PubMed Central (PMC) repository, and others. Conversely, MEDLINE offers more sophisticated search functions than PubMed, which could result in increasingly targeted results (U.S. National Library of Medicine, 2016).

In the end, theory-generating meta-synthesis researchers are urged to avoid conducting inexpert and redundant searches of both PubMed and MEDLINE, which tends to be time-intensive and results in many duplicate references. Instead, they are encouraged to learn about the advantages and disadvantages of both databases and make informed decisions about when it is most appropriate to search each one. For instance, in accordance with theoretical sampling, PubMed might be preferred when breadth is the goal, whereas MEDLINE might be favored when a more targeted search is in order.

Another notable database is Google Scholar, which is often used because of its widespread familiarity and its capacity to identify non-peer-reviewed literature. For several reasons, however, its utility is limited when conducting theory-generating meta-synthesis research. First, Google Scholar search functions are less sophisticated than those found within academic search engines, and there are fewer options for refining results. Thus, a single search can yield up to 1,000 viewable citations, but the first 50 to 100 tend to be the most relevant. Second, downloading large sets of results from Google Scholar to reference management software is challenging, if not impossible, and systematically eliminating duplicates and sorting citations can be difficult. Third, Google Scholar search algorithms are constantly changing, which means that search results cannot be easily replicated. Given these attributes, Google Scholar tends to be best suited for conducting one-time searches that are narrow or highly specific (Bramer, 2016; Guistini & Boulos, 2013; Pannabecker & Pardon, 2013; Shultz, 2007).

There are no rules regarding the number of reference databases that should be searched to complete a theory-generating meta-synthesis investigation. That said, in accordance with theoretical sampling and to ensure validity and generalizability of the findings, multiple topically relevant databases should be used. For instance, as part of an investigation of intimate partner violence among Native Americans, five cross-disciplinary databases were searched (i.e., CINAHL, GenderWatch, PubMed, Social Services Abstracts, and Social Work Abstracts [Finfgeld-Connett, 2015b]). The scope of each of these databases can be found in Table 3.1.

TABLE 3.1 Databases Searched for a Meta-synthesis Relating to Intimate Partner Violence Among Native Americans (Finfgeld-Connett, 2015b)

Database	Scope
CINAHL	Nursing and allied health
GenderWatch	Women and women's issues
PubMed	Biomedicine and health, including portions of the life sciences, behavioral sciences, chemical sciences, and bioengineering
Social Services Abstracts	Social work; human services; and related areas, such as social welfare, social policy, and community development
Social Work Abstracts	Social work

Searching the Literature

Theoretical Searching

Theory-generating meta-synthesis research calls for theoretical searching of the literature wherein search strategies are periodically broadened and narrowed to fully explicate a theory that is valid, contextually focused, and generalizable. Initial searches are guided by the research topic; however, they are often adapted as the topic is fine-tuned (Finfgeld-Connett & Johnson, 2013). For example, over the course of conducting a theory-generating meta-synthesis relating to intimate partner violence among Hispanic women, the search strategies were continuously fine-tuned to assemble a targeted sample of research reports relating to women of Mexican heritage who were living in the United States, legally or illegally (Finfgeld-Connett, 2017).

Search Terms

Researchers typically begin searching the literature by generating a comprehensive list of topically relevant search terms (e.g., Table 3.2) that are adapted to optimize the unique features of each reference database. For instance, Medical Subject Headings (i.e., MeSH Terms) should be used to maximize the number of relevant results within MEDLINE; whereas CINAHL, Embase, and PsycINFO each have their own unique set of subject headings.

Although universally accepted search terms for identifying qualitative versus quantitative research reports do not exist, CINAHL and PsycINFO offer filters to limit searches to qualitative research articles. When this feature is not available, researchers are advised to use search terms such as *qualitative* and *interview* to narrow their results to qualitative research articles (Flemming & Briggs, 2007; Gorecki, Brown, Briggs, & Nixon, 2010). Professionally designed search strategies (i.e., filters or hedges) for capturing qualitative research reports are available from the Hedges Project at McMaster University (http://hiru.mcmaster.ca/hiru/

TABLE 3.2 Initial Search Terms Relating to Women and Substance Abuse

Substance Abuse Terms	Gender-Specific Terms
Alcohol abuse★	Female★
Alcoholism★	Gender
Amphetamine★	Matern★
Cocaine	Mother★
Designer drugs	Parent★
Drug abuse	Pregnan★
Heavy drinker★	Woman
Heroin	Women
Illegal drug★	
Illicit drug★	
Inhalant abuse	
Marijuana	
Marihuana	
Meth	
Methamphetamine★	
Narcotic★	
Opiate★ abuse	
Opioid abuse	
Street drugs	
Substance abuse★	
Substance misuse	
Addiction	
Addict, Addicts	
AODA	
Drug offender★	

★*Note.* An asterisk (★) is applied to the end of a truncated search term so that all available forms of the word will be identified. For example, abuse★ will capture all forms of the term (e.g., abuses, abuser, etc.).

HIRU_Hedges_home.aspx); however, their precision and sensitivity are not always stable across searches (Flemming & Briggs, 2007).

All search strategies that are used to conduct a theory-generating meta-synthesis are part of the data collection process, and as such, they should be clearly dated and electronically stored along with the search results. Documented search strategies (see Table A3.1 in Appendix 2) comprise part of the research audit trail, which helps to make the research process transparent. Search strategies can be included in publications to help illustrate the research process, and they can also be used as a starting point if search results need to be updated (DeJean, Giacomini, Simeonov, & Smith, 2016).

Date Restrictions

Search results can be adapted based on publication dates, but cutoff points must be fully justified. For example, using an historical cutoff date is appropriate if a healthcare treatment strategy has changed due to an innovation (e.g., introduction of antiviral treatment for hepatitis C), and research findings prior to a certain point in time are no longer relevant (Barroso, Sandelowski, & Voils, 2006). Conversely, simply imposing cutoff dates to limit the number of results risks omitting relevant research reports and biasing the sample.

Language Restrictions

Although the vast majority of scientific research reports are published in English, when conducting context-specific theory-generating meta-syntheses, consideration should be given to including non-English language reports. For example, a research report written in the official language of Brazil (i.e., Portuguese) could be very valuable when researching birthing practices among Amazonian people. To ensure that context-specific meanings are captured, however, the expense of a translator must be factored into the overall cost of investigations that require this type of expertise (Toews et al., 2017; Van Weijen, 2012).

Backward and Forward Searching

Backward and forward citation searching is conducted once research reports have been selected for inclusion in the study sample. Backward, or ancestral searching, is accomplished by reviewing the reference lists of reports in the sample for similar types of documents. Forward searching, which is also called cited reference searching, involves identifying key documents and then searching forward in time for relevant reports in which they are cited (Finfgeld-Connett & Johnson, 2013). Both types of searching can be accomplished by using electronic databases such as Scopus, wherein the researcher can review both forward and backward citations along with their abstracts.

Key Author and Journal Searching

When experts in a topic area are identified, their names can be used to search for research reports that meet the study inclusion criteria. In addition, complete volumes of key journals can be searched online to identify articles that might have been overlooked using other search methods (Barroso et al., 2003; Finfgeld-Connett & Johnson, 2013). For example, when conducting a meta-synthesis relating to intimate partner violence, the *Journal of Family Violence, Journal of Interpersonal Violence*, and *Violence Against Women* were scanned online (Finfgeld-Connett, 2015a).

TOC Alerts

Theory-generating meta-synthesis investigations usually take months to complete. During this time, researchers can stay abreast of newly published articles that might meet the study inclusion criteria by signing up for table of contents alerts. These alerts are sent via email, and they include lists of early online publications as well as tables of contents of recently published journal issues. A tutorial for subscribing to TOC alerts through PubMed is available online (www. nlm.nih.gov/bsd/viewlet/myncbi/jourup/index.html). In addition, TOC alerts can be set up through publishers' websites (e.g., http://olabout.wiley.com/WileyCDA/Section/id-404511.html) or individual journal websites (e.g., http://wjn.sagepub.com/cgi/alerts).

Another method for staying up-to-date on topic-specific literature is to register for database updates. This can be accomplished by accessing a reference database (e.g., CINAHL, PsycINFO), creating an account, running a search, and requesting periodic (e.g., monthly) e-mail updates based on the same search strategy. Tutorials for setting up these types of email alerts can be accessed through academic library websites or through database websites (e.g., EBSCOhost: http://support.ebsco.com/knowledge_base/detail.php?id=4002)

Theoretical Sampling

When conducting theory-generating meta-synthesis research, theoretical sampling involves purposefully selecting research reports in accordance with the needs of theory development. Depending on the research topic and purpose, it might be possible to establish inclusion and exclusion criteria quite early during data collection, but researchers are urged to avoid setting limits prematurely because doing so could unnecessarily restrict theoretical sampling and theory development.

Depending on the scope of the research topic, searching the literature can result in hundreds if not thousands of citations that must be downloaded to reference management software. Reference management software, such as End-Note™, is ideal for efficiently removing duplicate citations prior to reviewing them for relevancy (Barroso et al., 2003). Thereafter, each article title and abstract should be scrutinized, and citations are included or excluded from the study database owing to topical relevancy and/or the research method. Occasionally, entire documents must be secured to determine if they meet the study inclusion criteria (see Figure 3.1).

Once included in the sample, reference management software such as End-Note™ can be used to categorize research reports based on any number of study attributes such as racial group, geography, culture, age, gender, and so forth (e.g., Screen Shot 3.1). Organizing references in this way is particularly helpful because the researcher can gauge which categories contain enough context-specific references to justify a theory-generating meta-synthesis. Depending on the volume of the search results, the job of sorting and culling citations can take weeks, and investigators are urged to reserve an adequate amount of time to carry out this important step of the research process.

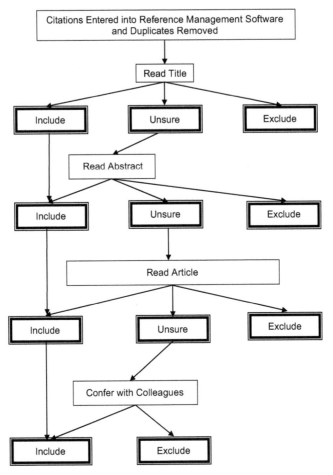

FIGURE 3.1 Research Report Selection

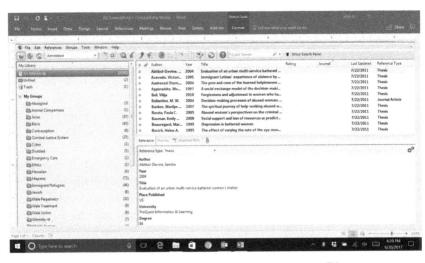

SCREEN SHOT 3.1 Organization of Report Citations in EndNote™

Quality Assessment of Research Reports

Assessment instruments, such as the Critical Appraisal Skills Program Checklist (see Appendix 5 [CASP, 2014]) are sometimes used to help researchers examine research reports for quality and potential inclusion in a meta-synthesis sample. Although this method is advocated by some meta-synthesis researchers, several cautionary notes are in order. First, these types of instruments cannot be used to evaluate an actual investigation. Rather, they can only be used to assess what was written about an investigation. Second, due to the diversity among qualitative research methods, judgments about quality run the risk of being biased. Third, the use of quality assessment instruments rarely results in the exclusion of research reports due to quality. Instead, investigators appear to primarily use them to familiarize themselves with the reports (Dalton, Booth, Noyes, & Sowden, 2017; Finfgeld-Connett, 2014; Sandelowski & Barroso, 2002; Thorne, 2009, 2017). Admittedly, the latter could be useful if researchers are not entirely familiar with qualitative methods, and/or the nature of qualitative research reports.

Qualitative research findings versus reports constitute the unit of analysis when conducting theory-generating meta-synthesis investigations (Finfgeld-Connett, 2014). Thus, instead of evaluating research reports for quality, investigators are urged to assess the validity of the raw data (i.e., qualitative research findings) during the data analysis process. Methods for doing this are discussed in Chapter 5.

Sample Size

The number of research reports that are necessary to complete a meta-synthesis investigation cannot be known from the outset (Finfgeld, 2003). Two key factors must be considered when deciding whether the literature will support a topically focused theory-generating meta-synthesis investigation. The first is whether there are enough research reports available to ensure validity. In general, the richer the raw data (i.e., primary qualitative research findings) the fewer the number of research reports that are required. For example, a theory relating to courage and the management of long-term health concerns was generated based on a sample of six rich research reports (Finfgeld, 1999). Conversely, a much larger sample (N = 60) was required to develop a model of perceived competency among homeless women with substance abuse problems (Finfgeld-Connett, Bloom, & Johnson, 2012). In part, the larger sample was required because many of the qualitative findings that were available for analysis were thinly described and/or the relationships among the categories or themes were not fully delineated.

Another factor to consider when estimating the number of research reports that are needed to conduct a theory-generating meta-synthesis investigation is whether multiple research reports have been generated from a single primary investigation. If so, findings from a single sample that are presented across several reports could give a false impression of triangulation. Moreover, if research findings are redundantly reported across reports, unjustified conclusions about saturation could be reached (Finfgeld, 2003).

Learning Activities

1. Complete an online tutorial pertaining to an academic reference database such as PubMed (www.nlm.nih.gov/bsd/disted/pubmed.html) or CINAHL (http://support.ebsco.com/cinahl/), and efficiently and effectively conduct a topical search of the qualitative literature.
2. Download the results of a topical search of the qualitative literature to reference management software such as EndNote™, remove duplicates, and categorize the remaining items (e.g., race, age, etc.).

Note

1 Sampling method that was developed by Glaser and Strauss (1967) to generate grounded theory.

References

Arksey, H., & O'Malley, L. (2005). Scoping studies: Towards a methodological framework. *International Journal of Social Research Methodology: Theory & Practice, 8*, 19–32. doi: 10.1080/1364557032000119616

Barroso, J., Gollop, C. J., Sandelowski, M., Meynell, J., Pearce, P. F., & Collins, L. J. (2003). The challenges of searching for and retrieving qualitative studies. *Western Journal of Nursing Research, 25*, 153–178. doi: 10.1177/0193945902250034

Barroso, J., Sandelowski, M., & Voils, C. I. (2006). Research results have expiration dates: Ensuring timely systematic reviews. *Journal of Evaluation in Clinical Practice, 12*, 454–462. doi: 10.1111/j.1365-2753.2006.00729.x

Bramer, W. M. (2016). Variation in number of hits for complex searches in Google Scholar. *Journal of the Medical Library Association: JMLA, 104*, 143–145. doi: 10.3163/1536-5050.104.2.009

Critical Appraisal Skills Programme (CASP). (2014). *Qualitative research checklist 31.05.13.* Retrieved from http://media.wix.com/ugd/dded87_29c5b002d99342f788c6ac670e49f274.pdf

Dalton, J., Booth, A., Noyes, J., & Sowden, A. J. (2017). Potential value of systematic reviews of qualitative evidence in informing user-centered health and social care: Findings from a descriptive overview. *Journal of Clinical Epidemiology.* Advance online publication. doi: 10.1016/j.jclinepi.2017.04.020

De Jean, D., Giacomini, M., Simeonov, D., & Smith, A. (2016). Finding qualitative research evidence for health technology assessment. *Qualitative Health Research, 26*, 1307–1317. doi: 10.1177/1049732316644429

EBSCO Support. (n.d.). *What is the difference between a "database" and an "interface?"* Retrieved from http://support.epnet.com/knowledge_base/detail.php?id=4162

Finfgeld, D. L. (1999). Courage as a process of pushing beyond the struggle. *Qualitative Health Research, 9*, 803–814. doi: 10.1177/104973299129122298

Finfgeld, D. L. (2003). Meta-synthesis: The state of the art—so far. *Qualitative Health Research, 13*, 893–904. doi: 10.1177/1049732303253462

Finfgeld-Connett, D. (2014). Use of content analysis to conduct knowledge-building and theory-generating qualitative systematic reviews. *Qualitative Research, 14*, 341–352. doi: 10.1177/1468794113481790

Finfgeld-Connett, D. (2015a). Intimate partner violence and its resolution among African American women. *Global Qualitative Nursing Research, 2*, 1–8. Retrieved from http://doi.org/10.1177/2333393614565182

Finfgeld-Connett, D. (2015b). Qualitative systematic review of intimate partner violence among Native Americans. *Issues in Mental Health Nursing, 36*, 754–760. doi: 10.3109/01612840.2015.1047072

Finfgeld-Connett, D. (2017). Intimate partner violence and its resolution among Mexican Americans. *Issues in Mental Health Nursing, 38*, 464–472. doi: 10.1080/01612840.2017.1284968

Finfgeld-Connett, D., Bloom, T. L., & Johnson, E. D. (2012). Perceived competency and resolution of homelessness among women with substance abuse problems. *Qualitative Health Research, 22*, 416–427. doi: 10.1177/1049732311421493

Finfgeld-Connett, D., & Johnson, E. D. (2013). Literature search strategies for conducting knowledge-building and theory-generating qualitative systematic reviews. *Journal of Advanced Nursing, 69*, 194–204. doi: 10.1111/j.1365-2648.2012.06037.x

Flemming, K., & Briggs, M. (2007). Electronic searching to locate qualitative research: Evaluation of three strategies. *Journal of Advanced Nursing, 57*, 95–100. doi: 10.1111/j.1365-2648.2006.04083.x

Giustini, D., & Boulos, M. N. K. (2013). Google Scholar is not enough to be used alone for systematic reviews. *Online Journal of Public Health Informatics, 5*(2), 1–9. Retrieved from http://dx.doi.org/10.5210/ojphi.v5i2.4623

Glaser, B. J., & Strauss, A. L. (1967). *The discovery of grounded theory: Strategies for qualitative research.* Hawthorne, NY: Aldine de Gruyter.

Gorecki, C. A., Brown, J. M., Briggs, M., & Nixon, J. (2010). Evaluation of five search strategies in retrieving qualitative patient-reported electronic data on the impact of pressure ulcers on quality of life. *Journal of Advanced Nursing, 66*, 645–652. doi: 10.1111/j.1365-2648.2009.05192.x

Macduff, C., Goodfellow, L., Leslie, G., Copeland, S., Nolfi, D., & Blackwood, D. (2016). Harnessing our rivers of knowledge: Time to improve nursing's engagement with electronic theses and dissertations. *Journal of Advanced Nursing, 72*, 2255–2258. doi: 10.1111/jan.12821

Pannabecker, V., & Pardon, K. (2013). *How do Google, Google Scholar, and other Google tools help health professionals navigate the oceans of information?* Poster Presentation at MLGSCA/NCNMLG Joint Meeting, 2013, UCSD, La Jolla, CA. Retrieved from https://repository.asu.edu/attachments/110702/content/Poster.pdf

Polit, D. F., & Beck, C. T. (2017). *Nursing research: Generating and assessing evidence for nursing practice* (10th ed.). Philadelphia, PA: Wolters Kluwer.

Sandelowski, M., & Barroso, J. (2002). Reading qualitative studies. *International Journal of Qualitative Methods, 1*, 74–108. Retrieved from https://ejournals.library.ualberta.ca/index.php/IJQM/article/download/4615/3764

Sandelowski, M., & Barroso, J. (2003). Classifying the findings in qualitative studies. *Qualitative Health Research, 13*, 905–923. doi: 10.1177/1049732303253488

Shultz, M. (2007). Comparing test searches in PubMed and Google Scholar. *Journal of the Medical Library Association, 95*, 442–445. doi: 10.3163/1536-5050.95.4.442

Thorne, S. (2009). The role of qualitative research within an evidence-based context: Can meta-synthesis be the answer? *International Journal of Nursing Studies, 46*, 569–575. doi: 10.1016/j.ijnurstu.2008.05.001

Thorne, S. (2017). Metasynthetic madness: What kind of monster have we created? *Qualitative Health Research, 27*, 3–12. doi: 10.1177/1049732316679370

Toews, I., Booth, A., Berg, R. C., Lewin, S., Glenton, C., Munthe-Kaas, H. M., . . . Meerpohl, J. J. (2017). Dissemination bias in qualitative research: Conceptual considerations. *Journal of Clinical Epidemiology*. Advance online publication. doi: 10.1016/j.jclinepi.2017.04.010

U.S. National Library of Medicine. (2016). Fact sheet. *MEDLINE, PubMed, and PMC (PubMed Central): How are they different?* Retrieved from www.nlm.nih.gov/pubs/factsheets/dif_med_pub.html

van Weijen, D. (2012, November). The language of (future) scientific communication. *Research Trends*, 31. Retrieved from www.researchtrends.com/issue-31-november-2012/the-language-of-future-scientific-communication/

4

DATA EXTRACTION, ANALYSIS, AND THEORY GENERATION

Deborah Finfgeld-Connett

The process of data extraction, analysis, and theory generation is covered in this chapter. Ways to identify and extract raw data from primary research reports are discussed. In addition, data coding, categorizing, memoing, and diagramming are explained along with strategies to ensure the validity of the resultant theory.

Overview of Data Extraction and Analysis

It is challenging to put qualitative methods into words, and written explanations tend to obfuscate the dynamic and creative nature of the process. As such, researchers are encouraged to study this chapter as necessary, but they are also urged to engage in data extraction and analysis as soon as possible. Until they do, there is no way to fully understand and hone the skills involved in data retrieval and analysis.

Rigorous methods are used to conduct theory-generating meta-synthesis research. That said, the process of qualitative data extraction and analysis is not rigid or lock-step, and variations occur depending on the aim of the research and the volume and quality of the data that are available. Variations also occur based on the unpredictable nature of the emergent findings.

When conducting theory-generating meta-synthesis research, two types of data are extracted from primary research reports for analysis: (a) qualitative findings and (b) characteristics of primary qualitative research investigations. Characteristics of primary qualitative research investigations (e.g., purpose, sample, methods) help investigators familiarize themselves with the sample, and they also help them to contextualize the research findings. Qualitative findings from primary research reports constitute the vast majority of the data, and analysis of these data results in the explication of theory (Finfgeld-Connett, 2014a). Extraction and analysis of these two types of data (i.e., characteristics of primary research investigations and qualitative findings) are discussed in the remainder of this chapter.

Study Characteristics: Extraction, Entry, and Analysis

Study characteristics include attributes such as the research purpose, theoretical framework, sample, and methods. To prepare to extract these data, research reports are read and study characteristics are highlighted. Prior to extracting information, a table should be formatted using word processing software. Reference citations are placed in the first column, and subsequent columns are labeled in accordance with the study attributes of interest (e.g., purpose, theoretical framework, sample, and methods). As data collection ensues, columns are added, deleted, or relabeled to accommodate the type of information that is pertinent and available for extraction (see template in Table 4.1 and Table A5.1 in Appendix 4).

Occasionally, meta-synthesis researchers contact authors of primary qualitative research reports to glean information about study characteristics (e.g., research design, method, and sample) that are not included in a research report. A productive line of inquiry often involves clarifying whether multiple research reports stem from a single sample. This is important because triangulation is diminished and saturation is compromised when more than one research report stems from a single investigation.

The benefits of contacting primary researchers aside, there are also potential problems involved in contacting authors of primary investigations. First, memories can be short, and/or knowledgeable informants might not be available. Second, researchers could feel compelled to cast their work in the best light possible, and they might provide biased responses. For example, if asked whether they used a research theoretical framework (e.g., grounded theory) to guide data collection and analysis, the authors might indicate that they did, when in fact they only used it to position their research within the qualitative paradigm.

Once study characteristics are extracted and placed within a table, analysis of this information consists of summarizing attributes across investigations.

TABLE 4.1 Template: Characteristics of Primary Qualitative Investigations

References	Purpose and Questions	Theoretical Framework	Sample				Methods	
			Geographic Location	Source of Sample	N = Women	N = Men	Data Collection	Data Analysis

Occasionally, quantitative calculations (e.g., sums, means) are warranted to analyze study samples. In these instances, quantitative data analysis software such as Microsoft Excel™ can be used.

Qualitative Findings: Data Extraction and Entry

The following methods for extracting and analyzing qualitative research findings have been successfully used with a sample as large as 60 (e.g., Finfgeld-Connett, Bloom, & Johnson, 2012). That said, when sample sizes exceed 25–30 research reports, data organization and manipulation can be challenging. In these instances, researchers could consider using qualitative data analysis software such as NVivo™ or Dedoose™, especially for coding and categorizing. With or without the use of software, the principles behind the methods that are described in this chapter apply.

Identifying and Locating the Data

Some investigators find it difficult to clearly identify primary qualitative research findings. To clarify, qualitative findings consist of fully analyzed results. Codes and categories, which are sometimes presented in tables, and unanalyzed quotations do not constitute qualitative research findings, and they are not considered raw data when conducting theory-generating meta-synthesis investigations.

To complicate matters, some investigators deviate from standard reporting formats, and findings can be found in several places, especially the discussion section (Sandelowski & Barroso, 2002a). Uncertainty about what constitutes qualitative findings is particularly problematic when isolated concepts are presented in the findings section, and dynamic links/relationships among concepts are described in the discussion. In these instances, researchers must determine whether the latter are mere suppositions or valid findings. To decide, investigators are urged to consider whether the authors explicated data analysis methods for inferring linkages/relationships among concepts or whether their methods are limited to thematically organizing or coding and categorizing raw data. If methods for systematically linking concepts (e.g., memoing, diagramming) are not discussed, it is likely that relationships among concepts that are mentioned in the discussion section are suppositions. Conversely, if methods for explicating links among concepts are clearly outlined, it is likely that conceptual relationships, no matter where they appear in the report, constitute valuable findings that should be extracted for analysis.

Data Extraction and Entry

Extraction of qualitative research findings begins after reading, studying, and making notations in the margins of one or two research reports. Based on the data that are available in this limited number of reports, tentative codes can be identified, and

TABLE 4.2 Template: Initial Coding

References	Code	Code	Code	Code	Code	Code
Reference 1	Raw Data	Raw Data	Raw Data	Raw Data	Raw Data	Raw Data
Reference 2	Raw Data	Raw Data	Raw Data	Raw Data	Raw Data	Raw Data
Reference 3	Raw Data	Raw Data	Raw Data	Raw Data	Raw Data	Raw Data
Reference 4	Raw Data	Raw Data	Raw Data	Raw Data	Raw Data	Raw Data

raw data can be preliminarily organized. In preparation for extracting qualitative findings for analysis, computer software should be used to format a table wherein reference citations are listed in the first column, and tentative codes are used to label subsequent columns (see template in Table 4.2). To avoid transcription errors, qualitative research findings should be electronically copied from research reports whenever possible and pasted into formatted tables (Finfgeld-Connett, 2014b).

To avoid decontextualizing research findings, it is important to extract qualitative findings in context. This means capturing full descriptions of findings, which can amount to one or two sentences or several paragraphs. Lengthier descriptions are often associated with findings that are part of theoretical frameworks, because concepts as well as their complex relationships must be captured (Finfgeld-Connett, 2014b).

In addition to potentially extracting decontextualized findings, there is the risk of capturing data segments that are too large to be easily analyzed in meaningful ways. This can result in overly abstract coding and findings that do not fully and precisely answer the research questions. One way to avoid this problem is to carefully mark and extract cohesive research findings rather than extracting multiple findings or fragments of multiple findings at one time (Finfgeld-Connett, 2014b).

Analysis and Synthesis of Qualitative Findings to Develop Theory

When conducting theory-generating meta-synthesis investigations, there are two ways to approach data analysis and synthesis. The first method is generally used when the purpose of the study is to develop an entirely new theory, and there are no preexisting assumptions about coding structures (e.g., see Finfgeld-Connett et al. [2012] in Appendix 2). The second method is used when the purpose of the investigation is to adapt an existing framework, and tentative ideas about how to code and categorize data exist from the outset (e.g., see Finfgeld-Connett [2017] in Appendix 4). The former situation is discussed first.

Coding and Categorizing

Consistent with grounded theory (Corbin & Strauss, 2008), data analysis should result in a process framework. Processes consist of fully developed concepts and their dynamic relationships; including antecedents, outcomes, and feedback loops.

As such, researchers are encouraged to keep this overarching model in mind as they code and categorize raw data (Finfgeld-Connett, 2014a, 2014b).

Initially, the goal of coding is to inductively organize raw data in a transparent manner, thus, early codes should remain close to the data. These concrete codes capture the essence of the raw data, and they range from single words to very short phrases. Often, a single strand of data relates to multiple ideas, and thus, it is associated with more than one code. If a single strand of data is associated with more than three codes, however, researchers are urged to examine whether they have captured multiple findings that need to be separated and analyzed individually (Finfgeld-Connett, 2014a, 2014b).

It is easy to get caught up in the relatively simple task of attaching transparent codes to raw data. Based on volume alone, however, this sort of coding can quickly become overwhelming. Thus, as soon as similarities and associations among codes are identified, coded data should be grouped across studies into subcategories and categories. Less concrete and more metaphorical codes are used to label these newly formulated subcategories and categories, which results in greater abstraction and generalizability of the findings (e.g., see Tables 4.3 and 4.4) (Finfgeld-Connett, 2014a, 2014b).

Subcategories and categories are formulated based on clustering, wherein particularized codes are iteratively grouped to develop more abstract metaphors (Miles & Huberman, 1994). Effectual metaphors are cohesive, and they clearly represent the particularities of the phenomenon under investigation. When clarity and/or cohesiveness is a problem, researchers are advised to return to the raw data to ensure that their subcategories and categories are firmly grounded. In most instances, unaltered metaphors will not be carried forward from primary research findings, because the goal is to push knowledge development forward. When this occurs, however, the origins of these metaphors must be clearly cited.

Coding structures quickly become large and unwieldy, and they must be sub-divided and placed into separate files (e.g., Word™) or worksheets (e.g., Excel™). Numerous files/worksheets are generally needed to accommodate all data analysis tables that are required to conduct a single investigation. As codes

TABLE 4.3 Template: Categorical and Subcategorical Coding

Category						
References	*Subcategory*		*Subcategory*			*Subcategory*	
Reference 1	Code	Code	Code	Code	Code	Code	Code
Reference 2	Raw Data	Raw Data	Raw Data	Raw Data	Raw Data	Raw Data	Raw Data
Reference 3	Raw Data	Raw Data	Raw Data	Raw Data	Raw Data	Raw Data	Raw Data
Reference 4	Raw Data	Raw Data	Raw Data	Raw Data	Raw Data	Raw Data	Raw Data

TABLE 4.4 Coded/Categorized Data: Intimate Partner Violence Among South Asian Immigrants (Finfgeld-Connett & Johnson, 2013)

Reference	Betrayal of Social Contract	Coping	Ineffective Coping		
			Rumination	Self and Other Blame	Somatization
Kallivayalil (2010)	Faith placed in: • Husband and his family • Arranged marriage system Felt cheated, tricked, and used by system and people who should have protected them	Focus on one positive outcome of marriage: children	Intense rumination and rewinding of their lives and marriage history • Search for explanations, meaning in suffering • Moral evaluations • Blame • Fatalism • Depression • Preoccupation with husbands, children, in-laws, parents, community members who are part of moral universe • Preoccupation with depressive and anxious themes	Self-blame for: • Trusting future husband and families • Not asking more questions Other blame: • Arranged marriage system • Immigration status • Western ways • Husband's anger Karma, destiny: Deserved abuse because of something in a former life	Culturally consistent to suppress mental distress and express it through physical complaints. Social service system makes it easier for women to be seen for physical but not psychological complaints.

and categories organically expand and contract, data analysis files/worksheets must be carefully labeled (e.g., attributes of core concepts, antecedents, and outcomes) to ensure that coding structures remain well organized.

Memoing

Coding and categorizing only represent a portion of the data analysis process that is required to inductively generate novel theory. Memoing is also needed to fully explicate concepts and the dynamic relationships among them. Failure to memo or incomplete memoing results in isolated concepts and/or partially explicated processes that have limited value. To avoid this problem, investigators are urged to begin developing inferential descriptions (i.e., memos) of concepts and the relationships among them after the findings from just two or three research reports have been coded and categorized (Finfgeld-Connett, 2014a, 2014b).

When conducting theory-generating meta-syntheses, two types of narrative memos are developed: within-study and cross-study memos. In the case of within-study memos, findings that have been extracted from primary research reports are carefully examined, and they are distilled into concise descriptive statements (see Table 4.5 column 3). These memos are subsequently compared and contrasted across studies, and similar statements are grouped together so that cross-study memos can be developed.

Cross-study memos are developed by carefully comparing and contrasting within-study memos across multiple primary research reports and gradually synthesizing them into a cohesive whole. Simply stated, this process involves iteratively and reflexively refining (i.e., translating, interpreting) within-study memos across studies until concepts and the dynamic relationships among them are fully explicated (see Table 4.5 columns 4 and 5).

Memoing can result in the articulation of many types of relationships among concepts, including linear, cyclical, convergent, divergent, and hierarchical (see Figure 4.1) (Finfgeld-Connett, 2014a, 2014b; Lempert, 2007). As rigorous memoing ensues, emergent relationships are continuously evaluated, revised, and reevaluated in accordance with the raw data. This type of memoing pushes synthesis forward, and it helps to ensure that valid, cohesive, and well-articulated elements of process theory (i.e., concepts and their dynamic relationships) are explicated (Birks, Chapman, & Francis, 2008; Finfgeld-Connett, 2014b) (see Table 4.5 column 5).

Memoing as the Primary Data Analysis Strategy

Instead of starting data analysis by coding and categorizing raw data, memoing is sometimes the primary data analysis strategy that is used. This is often the case when the research aim is to adapt an existing theoretical framework rather than to develop an entirely new one. In these situations, memoing is preferred over fine-grained coding and categorizing, because the latter could result in unnecessary deconstruction and de-contextualization of substantiated knowledge (Thorne, Jensen, Kearney, Noblit, & Sandelowski, 2004).

For example, memoing was the primary data analysis strategy when a theory-generating meta-synthesis was conducted in relationship to intimate partner violence among Mexican Americans (e.g., see Finfgeld-Connett [2017] in Appendix 4). In this case, the overall process of intimate partner violence was already well documented (e.g., Walker, 2017). Thus, the purpose of the meta-synthesis was to particularize this process within the context of a specific cultural group.

TABLE 4.5 Formative Category: Strategies for Resolving Intimate Partner Violence Among Native Americans (Finfgeld-Connett, 2015)

Formative Subcategory: Trust

1 Reference	2 Findings From Primary Sources	3 Within-Study Memos	4 Cross-Study Memos	5 Elements of Process Theory
Austin, Gallop, McCay, Peternelj-Taylor, and Bayer (1999)	Trust must be earned and not expected. Many nurses indicated a belief that, when working with First Nations people, it is crucial to try to learn about and understand their culture. They indicated, in particular, the role of spirituality, spiritual healing, the role of chiefs, the role of the extended family, and the role of women in the community. Nonverbal behaviors, such as avoiding direct eye contact, respecting and using silence, were identified as important. Most nurses believed that the challenge rested in the need for nurses to acquire ways to be helpful to First Nations people, rather than the necessity for First Nations people to adapt to the values and practices of mainstream health care.	Trust in service providers emerges over time. Service providers must learn about and accommodate Native American culture. Spirituality plays a role in the healing process. Tribal leaders, extended family, and women play a special role in the community. Service providers must understand customs relating to communication such as avoiding direct eye contact and respecting and using silence.	Native Americans perceive that lack of trust is a key barrier to seeking help. In part, this relates to the fact that service providers are uninformed about Native American culture (Austin et al., 1999; Burnette, 2013; Jones, 2008; Matamonasa-Bennett, 2013). Providers are urged to understand that non–Native American strategies that are used to resolve intimate partner violence are often viewed as coercive, domineering, and oppressive (Jones, 2008). Moreover, interventions that focus on power and control are incongruent with Native American values (Matamonasa-Bennett, 2013).	To effectively work with Native Americans to diminish intimate partner violence, service providers are urged to develop trusting relationships. They are encouraged to learn about Native American customs and to understand how they differ from the dominant culture's ways of doing things (Austin et al., 1999; Burnette, 2013; Jones, 2008; Matamonasa-Bennett, 2013). Intervention strategies that focus on power and control should be avoided (Jones, 2008; Matamonasa-Bennett, 2013). Instead, service providers are encouraged to leverage the support of tribal leaders, community members, and family (Austin et al., 1999).

Native American women lose trust in service agencies, because they are perceived to be ineffective. They report unprofessional, uninformed, and inconsistent responses from police. They also indicate that outside political forces affect how tribal leaders approach intimate partner violence (Burnette, 2013).

Service providers are encouraged to learn about roles that tribal leaders, spiritual leaders, extended family, and women traditionally play in Native American communities (Austin et al., 1999). They are also urged to follow tribal communication norms such as maintaining confidentiality, avoiding direct eye contact, and respecting and using silence (Austin et al., 1999; Burnette, 2013).

Police officers should behave professionally and act in consistent and unbiased ways (Burnette, 2013). Service providers are urged to observe interpersonal communication norms such as maintaining strict confidentiality, avoiding direct eye contact, and respecting and using silence (Austin et al., 1999; Burnette, 2013).

(Continued)

TABLE 4.5 (Continued)

1 *Reference*	*2* *Findings From Primary Sources*	*3* *Within-Study Memos*	*4* *Cross-Study Memos*	*5* *Elements of Process Theory*
Burnette (2013)	Lack of standardized response to violent crimes was a problem. Lack of significant sanctioning against abuse. Confidentiality was a priority of paramount importance. Half of women were concerned about confidentiality across formal service agencies. Women did not seek out services for fear their information would not be kept confidential, and some women reported that confidentiality was breached. Confidentiality in a tight-knit community, where everyone knew everyone, was a problem across formal systems. Many women felt uncomfortable seeking help from people they knew for issues related to intimate partner violence. The cumulative effect of an ineffective response from the formal system, an unsupportive family, as well as tangible barriers might keep women with their abusive partners, might keep them from seeking services, and might make them feel like there was no way out.	To establish trust, confidentiality must be ensured. Native Americans live in tight-knit communities, and they are uncomfortable seeking assistance from people they know. Native women lose trust in service agencies because they perceive that they have routinely failed them. They feel victimized by intimate partners as well as by the formal system that is supposed to help them. Women report multiple problems such as unprofessional, uninformed, and inconsistent responses from police and the tribal justice system.		

Not only did women feel violated by their abuser, some women felt punished by social services who they felt lacked a holistic understanding of the intimate partner violence situation.

Women tended to feel punished for factors associated with intimate partner violence that they felt were out of their control, such as housing issues.

Women reported negative experiences with the formal system, which may inadvertently perpetuate oppressions by imposing multiple victimizations.

Women reported multiple problems including most perpetrators fleeing before the police arrived, the lack of a standardized response from the police and tribal justice system, insignificant sanctioning for crimes of IPV, a lack of training, and a need for professionalism and accountability.

When professionals did favors for perpetrators with political power or with whom they had personal relationships, women were left feeling unsafe and without justice.

Women feel unsafe and without recourse because professionals tend to do favors for politically influential tribal members.

(Continued)

TABLE 4.5 (Continued)

1 Reference	2 Findings From Primary Sources	3 Within-Study Memos	4 Cross-Study Memos	5 Elements of Process Theory
Jones (2008)	Low levels of cultural sensitivity could lead to a lack of trust, and unwillingness by Native Americans to use services. Many Native Americans will not seek help because of fear or lack of trust in service providers. An example of a culturally inappropriate intervention given by an informant concerned an educational consultant who had been hired by a social agency to develop a program to stem the high rate of school drop-outs among local Native American youth. The consultant suggested linking the receipt of casino allotments to school attendance. Workers at the agency were furious at the suggestion. The intervention was seen as too much interference in personal autonomy, overly oppressive, and reflective of the way the dominant culture coercively deals with Indians.	Native Americans do not trust helping agencies because they are uninformed about tribal culture. Outside interventions to curtail intimate partner violence are viewed as coercive, domineering, and oppressive.		
Matamonasa-Bennett (2013)	The men who had participated in treatment by professionals indicated that it was a negative experience due to racial differences and issues of trust. Professional treatment that emphasized power and control issues in domestic violence was "out of tune" with traditional Native values. Racial and cultural differences are important in treatment.	Native American men perceive that cultural differences and lack of trust are barriers to treatment. Treatment that focuses on power and control issues is incongruent with Native American values.		

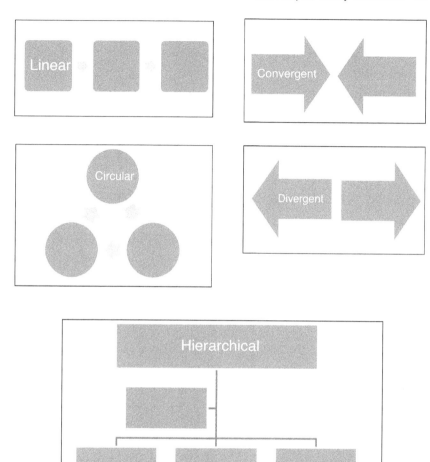

FIGURE 4.1 Examples of Dynamic Relationships Among Concepts

When memoing is the principle data analysis strategy, researchers begin analysis from a hypothetical-deductive stance. Qualitative research findings are extracted from research reports, and they are subsequently distilled into concise descriptive statements (see Table 4.6). Based on tentative coding categories (see Table 4.7), these within-study memos are then categorically grouped across studies. Metaphorical labels are applied to grouped memos, and cross-study memoing continues until refined results are generated (see Table 4.8). Based on this reflexive and iterative data analysis process, well-developed concepts and their inter-relationships are translated across studies, and a context-specific theory is formulated.

TABLE 4.6 Development of Within-study Memos: Intimate Partner Violence and Its Resolution Among Mexican Americans (Finfgeld-Connett, 2017)

1 References	2 Qualitative Findings	3 Within-study Memos
Belknap and Sayeed (2003)	Women indicated they would talk with their parents, sister, or a good friend. They specifically described sisters and friends who understood their situation, either because they knew them quite well or because they themselves were in similar situations.	Women tend to disclose to parents, sisters, or close friends. If none of these individuals is available, women are likely to remain silent.
	If your family is not nearby, or if you do not have a good friend, then you talk to no one. A series of questions and prompts was used to find out whether women had been asked about abuse, violence, or similar problems in their lives. Each said she had never been asked such questions.	No one, including health-care professionals, is likely to inquire about abuse. This is despite the fact that women approve of such inquiries, and some would feel comfortable providing candid answers to individuals who expressed a sincere interest and were trustworthy.
	Women were asked what they thought about being asked by a doctor or nurse about abuse. Most of the women responded that they thought it would be good to be asked. Although none of the women had experienced being asked such a question, five women indicated that they would answer openly.	
	Two women indicated that they would be afraid to answer such a question truthfully if there was abuse and that other women also might have reasons to be afraid to answer such a question truthfully. However, these women did not entirely reject the notion that health-care providers might ask the question.	Trust tends to develop over time, so it is important to ask about abuse more than once.
	Listening was described consistently throughout the narratives as very important in contributing to the woman's confidence to discuss her situation. Not listening was specifically described as inhibiting.	
	Women said they felt they could talk with nurses and doctors who showed an interest in their lives.	Mexican immigrant women might have very limited access to health care, and they might only seek care for their children. Thus, it might be valuable to ask women about abuse when they accompany their children for care.
	Building trust is a process that may take more than one interaction with the health-care provider, supporting the practice of asking every woman on every visit about abuse and violence.	
	The women in this study had very limited access to health care, most frequently accessing health care for their children rather than for themselves, supporting the inclusion of screening questions for the mother during clinic visits for the children.	

Adames and Campbell (2005)	In general, immigrant Latinas in their community do not have good relationships with their partners.	Women identified multiple types of abuse, including physical, verbal, emotional, psychological, and sexual.
	Most of the participants attributed the current negative state of intimate relationships in their community to men's behaviors or sociocultural pressures. Specifically, six of the women identified men's control over women and machismo as reasons why relationships between immigrant Latinas in their community and their partners are not good, and three of the women described immigration changes as elements that strain intimate relationships. Other reasons (mentioned by only one participant) included men's violence toward women, men's alcohol and drug use, social pressure on women to attend to men, pressure to be or stay married, and distress experienced by immigrant Latinas in their community because of the bad conditions of their relationships.	Consequences of IPV include depression, lack of interest, and low self-esteem.
		Women learn about IPV through their own experiences, the experiences of others around them, public media, and social service organizations.
	The women in this study recognized that the lack of harmony in their intimate relationships is associated with factors that are extrinsic to immigrant Latinas. For example, male domination, machismo, and men's inability to cope with changes related to immigration were cited as reasons for poor quality relationships in their community.	For women, precursors of IPV include aggressive or abusive families, immigration experiences, customs, the value and respect given to women, bad luck, fear, lack of knowledge about relationships, and poor knowledge of options.
	Each of the immigrant Latinas in this study understood the circumstances of her intimate relationship not solely as a unique experience rooted in individual characteristics but more as a collective experience originating from systematic gender inequity.	IPV is a machismo way to deal with stress.
	Immigrant Latinas identified the various kinds of IPV. The most common types of abuse identified were physical and verbal violence, which were discussed by all of the women. Emotional, sexual, and the generic term *mistreatment* were each referred to by three of the women.	Intimate relationships among Mexican immigrants are subject to socio-cultural pressures: machismo, male domination, alcohol, and drug use. Men find it difficult to cope with changes related to immigration.
	Participants talked about alcohol as an antecedent or co-occurring element of IPV, and one woman also mentioned machismo. Consequences of IPV, such as depression, lack of interest, and lowered self-esteem were also identified by one of the participants.	Women experience institutionalized (socially based) gender inequity and violent family systems. There is pressure on women to attend to men and stay married.
	The participants inconsistently used categorical labels (such as physical, verbal, emotional, psychological, sexual) or specific behaviors (such as hitting, insulting, changing the way you think).	

(Continued)

TABLE 4.6 (Continued)

1 *References*	*2* *Qualitative Findings*	*3* *Within-study Memos*
	Specific behaviors included hitting; threatening; keeping at home; dominating, controlling or manipulating; hurting with words or actions; pushing or pulling; oppressing; disdaining; insulting; offending with ugly or bad words; making them feel guilty or believe bad things; changing the way they think or act; and coercing or forcing sex.	Being an immigrant can be stressful, because gender expectations are different in new locations. Familial social support systems are disrupted, and women have limited knowledge of social services.
	All of the immigrant Latinas indicated that they learned about IPV mostly through their own experiences or by witnessing the experiences of others around them as well as through television media. Four of the women also gave credit to social service organizations they had come in contact with since coming to the United States. None of the participants identified parents or other relatives as sources of information about IPV unless their relative had actually been involved in incidents that the women had seen or heard about. Learning about IPV through diversified means (private experiences, public media, and social service organizations) provided the women a broader understanding of IPV than when they would have had if they had relied solely on the points of view of a single source of information.	Some women find that a more socially progressive environment encourages them to challenge their partners and families of origin.
	The more common types of abuse emerged, such as physical and verbal violence, followed by emotional, sexual, and the generic mistreatment. What was new in this third part of the participants' knowledge about IPV were references made to "control [of men over women]" by three of the women.	
	They acknowledge IPV as a systemic or institutionalized problem, rather than perceiving it as an individually determined phenomenon.	
	Immigrant Latinas in this study easily identified physical and verbal aggression as abusive, yet they did not readily recognize sexual and emotional aggression as abusive.	
	All of the participants affirmed that in their community immigrant Latinas are abused by their partners and that dealing with abusive partners is a problem faced by women throughout the Latino community.	

Participants attributed responsibility to environmental factors, such as aggressive or abusive families, immigration experiences, customs, the value or respect given to women, and the lack of knowledge about relationships. Additionally, three of the participants associated IPV in their community with men's behaviors or attitudes, such as IPV being a mechanism to cope with stress or being linked to machismo. Last, three participants also related IPV to women's luck, fear, and poor knowledge of their options.

The women in this study acknowledged the effect that sociocultural pressures have on the experiences of immigrant Latinas experiencing IPV. Specifically, the participants linked male domination, machismo, and men's inability to cope with changes related to immigration to the lack of harmony in their intimate relationships. They also associated the prevalence of IPV in their community with other extrinsic factors, such as violent family systems, immigrant experiences, traditions, the value attributed to women, men's inability to cope with stress, and male domination. Thus, the participants make reference to the various means through which inequalities between men and women are created and sustained within their families and their community at large. Disparities in the rights and obligations of men and women that are inculcated since childhood shape the gender roles that immigrant Latinos in this community adhere to as adults.

For some of the immigrant Latinas in this study, coming to the United States has provided alternative ways of thinking about gender roles and power dynamics. These women viewed being an immigrant as an advantage because they find themselves in a socially progressive environment that supports their opinions and encourages them to use their knowledge to challenge their partners and families. On the other hand, other women considered being an immigrant a disadvantage, given the poor immediate social support network (i.e., the absence of relatives and friends), misinformation about entitlement to services, and stress in intimate relationships that may include shifts in gender roles.

TABLE 4.7 Tentative Coding Categories: Intimate Partner Violence and Its Resolution Among Mexican Americans (Finfgeld-Connett, 2017)

Abuse as a Way of Life
Types of Abuse and Its Effects
Precursors of Abuse
Barriers to Resolving Abuse
Resolution of Intimate Partner Violence
Helping Strategies
Outcomes

It is important to note that when researchers start an investigation with pre-conceived ideas about how memoing should progress, there is a risk that novel data will be overlooked, and prevailing ideas will simply be verified rather than enhanced. This is likely to occur, because it is easier to verify conventional wisdom rather than to recognize and understand experiences and perspectives that fall outside of the norm (Onwuegbuzie & Leech, 2007; Thorne, 2017). This threat to validity and ways to avoid it are discussed later in this chapter (Finfgeld-Connett, 2014b).

Diagramming

Regardless of whether memoing is preceded by fine-grained coding and catego-rizing, diagrams (i.e., figures) should be created throughout the data analysis process to illustrate emergent concepts and how they dynamically relate or fit together. Diagramming provides a visual way of staying reflexively engaged so that the data can be more fully and accurately analyzed and synthesized. Dia-grams help researchers identify conceptual and relational gaps in models. They also help researchers recognize when concepts and the linkages among them are unclear. Moreover, they help researchers identify when data synthesis is incom-plete. In the latter instance, diagrams tend to appear unwieldy and confusing, because concepts are not fully synthesized, and relationships among them are not fully and accurately articulated (Buckley & Waring, 2013; Finfgeld-Connett, 2014b).

To ensure the generation of a process model, concepts, including antecedents and outcomes of phenomena, should be chronologically positioned within dia-grams. Formative diagramming does not require sophisticated software or artistic ability. Instead, initial diagrams often amount to primitive line drawings, sketches, or sticky notes that are assembled in a notebook or on a flipchart. A key advan-tage of these types of diagrams is that they can be easily shared with mentors and colleagues, who can help to pinpoint problem areas without spending an inordinate amount of time reviewing codes, categories, and/or memos. Over

TABLE 4.8 Within and Cross-study Memos: Intimate Partner Violence and Its Resolution Among Mexican Americans (Finfgeld-Connett, 2017)

Category: Abuse as a Way of Life

Within-Study Memos	Cross-Study Memo
For women, precursors of IPV include aggressive or abusive families, immigration experiences, customs, the value and respect given to women, bad luck, fear, lack of knowledge about relationships, and little knowledge of options (Adames & Campbell, 2005).	It is not uncommon for abused Mexican American women to be repeatedly mistreated by family members and friends (Adames & Campbell, 2005; Davila & Brackley, 1999; Divin et al., 2013; Fuchsel, 2013; Kim et al., 2017; Liendo et al., 2011; Mattson & Ruiz, 2005; Montalvo-Liendo et al., 2009).
Women tend to have a long history of physical, psychological, and sexual abuse (Davila & Brackley, 1999).	
Childhood abuse by parents and extended family members is common. Women leave their families of origin early to escape abuse only to cyclically reexperience it with intimate partners (Divin, Volker, & Harrison, 2013).	
Women who experience childhood sexual abuse are at greater risk of experiencing domestic violence as adults (Fuchsel, 2013).	
Families of origin are viewed ambivalently. Women often feel rejected and emotionally abused by them, but they can also be supportive during the process of immigrating to the United States (Kim, Draucker, Bradway, Grisso, & Sommers, 2017).	
It is not uncommon for women to have been repeatedly abused throughout their lives by family members and friends, as well as by individuals in the criminal justice system. Members of their partners' families can be abusers, and their own children sometimes mimic the abuse they have witnessed and endured (Liendo, Wardell, Engebretson, & Reininger, 2011).	
IPV is fueled by a family history of abuse, alcohol use, and women's reluctance to leave because they do not perceive that they have anywhere to go. Women also remain in the home for religious and financial reasons, and because, in the short run, they view it as the best thing for their children (Mattson & Ruiz, 2005).	
Mexican immigrant women are exceedingly vulnerable to IPV, because it is often normalized within their families of origin (Montalvo-Liendo, Wardell, Engebretson, & Reininger, 2009).	

(Continued)

TABLE 4.8 (Continued)

Category: Abuse as a Way of Life

Within-Study Memos	Cross-Study Memo
Many migrant women do not consider their intimate partners friends or lovers. Often, they feel forced to marry men that they have not known very long due to their legal status, loneliness, or pregnancy. In keeping with Mexican culture, a woman feels committed to a man once she has had sex with him (Fuchsel, Murphy, & Dufresne, 2012).	Women are apt to leave their nuclear families early, marry, and reexperience abuse with their intimate partners. Among women who are sexually abused by non-family members, cultural mores tend to obligate them to marry the perpetrators, and the cycle of abuse continues (Fuchsel, 2012; Divin et al., 2013; Kim et al., 2017).
Childhood abuse by parents and extended family members is common. Women leave their families of origin early to escape abuse only to cyclically reexperience it with intimate partners (Divin et al., 2013).	
Premarital virginity is highly valued. Women who are sexually abused as children (often by immediate family members) or raped by intimate partners are considered whores by their partners, families, and community. These individuals are subject to being rejected by their families of origin, kicked out of the house, and forced to marry the abuser (Kim et al., 2017).	

Category: Precursors of Abuse

Within-study Memos	Cross-study Memo
For women, precursors of IPV include aggressive or abusive families, immigration experiences, customs, the value and respect given to women, bad luck, fear, lack of knowledge about relationships, and little knowledge of options (Adames & Campbell, 2005).	Within Mexican American culture, intimate partner violence is fueled by machismo, wherein men are expected to be paternalistic, domineering, and controlling (Adames & Campbell, 2005; Davila & Brackley, 1999; Grzywacz et al., 2009; Kyriakakis et al., 2012; Mattson & Ruiz, 2005). Conversely, women are expected to be subservient, and to take care of the home and family (Grzywacz et al., 2009; Kyriakakis et al., 2012; Montalvo-Liendo et al., 2009; Moya et al., 2014).
IPV is a machismo way to deal with stress (Adames & Campbell, 2005).	
Intimate relationships among Mexican immigrants are subject to socio-cultural pressures such as machismo, male domination, alcohol, and drug use. Men find it difficult to cope with changes related to immigration (Adames & Campbell, 2005).	
Women experience institutionalized (socially based) gender inequity and violent family systems. There is pressure on women to attend to men and stay married (Adames & Campbell, 2005).	

Women tend to have a long history of physical, psychological, and sexual abuse (Davila & Brackley, 1999).

In terms of social and sexual relationships with men, women report a lack of power (Davila & Brackley, 1999).

Due to the Mexican cultural tradition of machismo, women are encouraged to stay within the home, be subservient, and limit their interactions with unrelated men. To make ends meet, this arrangement does not work well in the United States (Grzywacz, Rao, Gentry, Marín, & Arcury, 2009).

Men draw on patriarchal standards that call for women to respect and obey them, manage the household and children, maintain their beauty, and meet their sexual needs (Kyriakakis, Dawson, & Edmond, 2012).

Women were only allowed to work outside the home when it was necessary for survival. Often, they were forced to surrender paychecks to their husbands (Kyriakakis et al., 2012).

Mexican men tend to recognize physical abuse, whereas, women recognize both physical and psychological abuse. From childhood, both men and women view physical violence as male machismo, which results in control of the woman (Mattson & Ruiz, 2005).

In Mexico, IPV goes unpunished (Mattson & Ruiz, 2005).

Religious beliefs and marianismo hold women to the convention that they should be conciliatory and submissive to keep the family together. In the United States, these cultural traditions clash with notions of gender equality and the fact that women might have more job opportunities than men (Mattson & Ruiz, 2005).

IPV is fueled by a family history of abuse, alcohol use, and women's reluctance to leave because they do not perceive that they have anywhere to go. Women also remain in the home for religious and financial reasons, and because, in the short run, they view it as the best thing for their children (Mattson & Ruiz, 2005).

Mexican immigrant women are exceedingly vulnerable to IPV because it is often normalized within their families of origin (Montalvo-Liendo et al., 2009).

Within Mexican culture, women are socialized to be caretakers of the family and household (Moya, Chávez-Baray, & Martínez, 2014).

(Continued)

TABLE 4.8 (Continued)

Category: Precursors of Abuse

Within-study Memos	Cross-study Memo
Women's paid employment causes tension in domestic relationships, which requires renegotiation of roles within the family. Women feel empowered by their newly acquired discretionary funds, the opportunity to make decisions, and their ability to access supportive networks and services. Simultaneously, they have less time for childrearing and household tasks, and they become frustrated by their husbands' refusal to help (Grzywacz et al., 2009).	When Mexican American women enter the United States, they are often forced to seek employment outside of the home to make ends meet (Grzywacz et al., 2009; Kyriakakis et al., 2012). This upsets the traditional family structure, and Mexican American men are forced to share their roles as family breadwinners and decision makers. Mexican American men must adjust to losing power and control, and they must also adapt to receiving less time and attention from their wives (Adames & Campbell, 2005; Grzywacz et al., 2009). To ease their distress, some Mexican American men resort to extra-marital affairs and/or alcohol and drug abuse (Adames & Campbell, 2005; Fuchsel et al., 2012; Kyriakakis et al., 2012; Mattson & Ruiz, 2005).
Men are frustrated and angered by the loss of their roles as sole breadwinners and decision makers within the home. They feel a loss of power and respect, and they resent that their wives have less time to manage the household and cater to their needs. Moreover, when men attempt to help out, they perceive that their partners are dissatisfied with their attempts (Grzywacz et al., 2009).	
Women were only allowed to work outside the home when it was necessary for survival. Often, they were forced to surrender paychecks to their husbands (Kyriakakis et al., 2012).	
Intimate relationships among Mexican immigrants are subject to socio-cultural pressures. Machismo, male domination, alcohol, and drug use. Men find it difficult to cope with changes related to immigration (Adames & Campbell, 2005).	
Machismo can result in extra-marital affairs, which women often accept as part of Mexican culture (Fuchsel et al., 2012).	
Religious beliefs and marianismo hold women to the convention that they should be conciliatory and submissive to keep the family together. In the United States, these cultural traditions clash with notions of gender equality and the fact that women might have more job opportunities than men (Mattson & Ruiz, 2005).	

Category: *Resolution of Intimate Partner Violence*

Within-study Memos	Cross-study Memo
Women tend to disclose to parents, sisters, or close friends. If none of these individuals is available, women are likely to remain silent (Belknap & Sayeed, 2003).	Mexican American women will disclose abuse to receptive family members who have the potential to help (Belknap & Sayeed, 2003). Families that live far away might be limited to providing emotional support; however, those who live close by often provide refuge, money, food, and/or clothing (Kyriakakis, 2014). When family members are not available, Mexican American women will turn to women friends. Trusted friends serve as role models, and they provide the encouragement and support that is needed to help Mexican American women resolve intimate partner violence. (Belknap & Sayeed, 2003; Kyriakakis, 2014; Liendo et al., 2011; Montalvo-Liendo et al. 2009).
Parents who live close to their daughters assist by providing a safe refuge, money, food, clothing, and emotional support. Those who live farther away (e.g., Mexico) are largely limited to providing emotional support. Sometimes a sibling is dispatched to the United States to help (Kyriakakis, 2014).	
Women will sometimes turn to friends for help to avoid revictimization by their family members (Liendo et al., 2011).	
Often, women disclose to friends before family. Friends generally offer support and instill confidence in women. There is a mutual sense of trust (Montalvo-Liendo et al., 2009).	
At first, women might just seek validation. They might not seek advice about what to do (Montalvo-Liendo et al., 2009).	
Within Mexican culture, sharing problems outside of the family is taboo, and women worry about gossip in the community. When family members are not available, however, Mexican women will share concerns about abuse with friends. With the encouragement and support of female friends, women will take bold steps such as call the police, obtain protection orders, and file for child support. They rely on women friends to be role models (Kyriakakis, 2014).	When they begin to disclose to others, Mexican American women might merely seek validation that their situations are intolerable, and that there is hope for improvement. Later, they are likely to ask for advice about what to do (Montalvo–Liendo et al., 2009). The latter can lead to taking actions such as calling the police, obtaining protection orders, and filing for child support (Kyriakakis, 2014; Ingram et al., 2010). Rarely, however, do these initial efforts lead immediately to the resolution of intimate partner violence.
Very few women directly inquire about Violence Against Women Act (VAWA) self-petition. Awareness of VAWA self-petition tends to occur over time, and information can come from friends of the family or neighbors in their informal immigrant network. Occasionally, information comes from church communities, counselors, first responders, or child service agencies such as Head Start (Ingram et al., 2010).	
Women tend to pursue legal assistance to inquire about a divorce or other services, and they subsequently learn about the option to gain legal immigration status for themselves and her children without their abusers knowing (Ingram et al., 2010).	

(Continued)

TABLE 4.8 (Continued)

Category: Resolution of Intimate Partner Violence

Within-study Memos	*Cross-study Memo*
Women often separate from their partners for weeks to months when physical, emotional, or psychological abuse impacts their children, and then they return (Fuchsel et al., 2012).	Instead, intimate partners are likely to repeatedly coax women to return home and to retract legal allegations before Mexican American women take definitive action (Fuchsel et al., 2012; Montalvo-Liendo et al., 2009).
Challenges arise after women disclose to police, and their partners coerce them to retract their statements (Montalvo-Liendo et al., 2009).	During the process of resolving intimate partner violence, women note that participating in faith communities or independent spiritual practices can help to sustain them (Divin et al., 2013; Dovydaitis, 2011). They also note that therapy can be helpful, especially if it focuses on traumatic events that have occurred throughout their lives (Dovydaitis, 2011). Once they feel more stable, Mexican American women tend to invest in themselves by getting an education, improving their language skills, finding employment, and developing relationships with new partners (Dovydaitis, 2011; Kim et al., 2017).
Although some women are conflicted about God's role in their plight, on the whole, faith communities and prayer tend to help women cope with abuse. Women pray to forget, forgive, and to be forgiven; but mostly, they pray for strength and an end to their suffering (Divin et al., 2013).	
Sustained work, therapy, faith in God, family support, and new non-abusive partners enhance the process of healing (Dovydaitis, 2011).	
Therapy that targets traumatic events that have permeated their lives is recommended (Dovydaitis, 2011).	
Women are focused on getting ahead by migrating, separating from abusive partners, learning English, getting an education, and obtaining financial and personal independence. Women find that they must become self-oriented versus other-oriented to improve their lives (Dovydaitis, 2011).	
Immigrating to the United States is seen as a way to get ahead financially, separate from abusive partners, and become independent. Women value learning to speak English and getting more education. Women become more self-oriented versus other oriented (Kim et al., 2017).	
Greater self-orientation can lead to finding new non-abusing partners and experiencing mutually gratifying sex (Kim et al., 2017).	

time, computer software such as Microsoft Word™ should be used to iteratively revise diagrams until the research findings are fully, yet concisely, illustrated (Buckley & Waring, 2013; Finfgeld-Connett, 2014b).

Both memos and diagrams, along with tables of coded and categorized data, constitute an audit trail of the data analysis process so that the provenance of the research findings is transparent. Polished memos and diagrams (see Figure A4.1 in Appendix 3 and Figure A5.1 in Appendix 4) serve as the basis for writing up the findings section of formal research reports, and finalized diagrams can be included in research reports to provide readers with a snapshot of the findings (Finfgeld-Connett, 2014b).

Validity

Validity refers to the trustworthiness of research findings. In the case of theory-generating meta-synthesis research, validity specifically relates to the trustworthiness or credibility of the resultant theory. Throughout the research process several strategies are used to enhance validity, including unbiased data collection and sampling, triangulation, and reflexivity.

It should be noted that when conducting theory-generating meta-synthesis research, research reports are not evaluated for quality. In part, this relates to the fact that the actual research cannot be assessed. Only the contents of the research report can be evaluated. Moreover, findings from qualitative research reports can only be superficially critiqued, and assessments are subjective and could be biased (Finfgeld-Connett, 2014b; Sandelowski & Barroso, 2002b; Thorne, 2009). Instead of assessing research reports for quality, several other methods are used to ensure the validity of meta-synthesis-generated theory. These methods are discussed next.

Unbiased Data Collection and Sampling

Validity of meta-synthesis-generated theory is ensured based on unbiased data collection and sampling methods. These methods include using well-justified criteria (e.g., cutoff dates) to expertly search across databases for commercially and non-commercially (e.g., government) published research reports. They also include systematically exploring the literature using cited reference, ancestral, author, and key journal search strategies. Establishing table of contents alerts (TOC) ensures that newly published research reports are not overlooked, and the use of theoretical sampling strategies helps to eliminate gaps in the resultant theory. See Chapter 3 for additional information about these data collection and sampling methods.

Triangulation

When conducting theory-generating meta-synthesis research, validity is also enhanced owing to the convergence of three forms of triangulation: (a) researcher, (b) theoretical, and (c) methodological. By default, primary qualitative investigations that comprise the sample of meta-synthesis investigations are conducted by many investigators who use multiple theoretical frameworks and a variety of research methods to generate findings. These factors alone help to ensure a thorough and unbiased examination of a research topic.

When conducting theory-generating meta-syntheses, triangulation also occurs when a diverse team of researchers collaboratively works to diminish bias and enhance rigor. As a group, these individuals bring multiple research experiences and perspectives to a project to promote sound decision-making in relationship to searching for primary research reports. They also help to ensure that sample inclusion and exclusion criteria are fully rationalized and equitably applied. Moreover, they systematically work to develop and implement rigorous protocols for identifying, extracting, and coding/categorizing raw data. Subsequently, they have the potential to promote the development of clear descriptive memos and the articulation of complex processes (Finfgeld, 2003).

The advantages of teamwork aside, two points of clarification are in order. First, a synchronous approach, wherein all researchers continuously dialogue and work together, helps to maximize triangulation. This contrasts with a piecemeal or assembly line approach wherein individuals are assigned to complete specific tasks (e.g., collect, extract, code/categorize data; memo, or diagram). Using the latter model, team members are precluded from simultaneously and holistically understanding the entirety of the research process, which is necessary to optimize researcher triangulation.

Second, to optimize triangulation, team members must be committed to egalitarian sharing and negotiation. Otherwise, one or two individuals are likely to dominate decision-making. To avoid this problem, researchers are urged to preemptively evaluate hierarchical relationships and power-dynamics among team members so that unbiased decision-making guidelines can be established and maintained throughout the research process.

Reflexivity

Reflexivity is another strategy that is used to ensure validity when conducting theory-generating meta-syntheses. Reflexivity involves critically considering one's own perspectives to ensure that personal biases do not influence data collection and analysis (Berger, 2013; Polit & Beck, 2017). For example, during data collection, researchers must continually reflect on whether they are including or excluding research reports based on presumptions about key search terms, discipline-specific databases, historical cutoff dates, and so forth.

Throughout the data analysis process, researchers reflexively evaluate codes, subcategories, categories, memos, and diagrams for accuracy and clarity; and changes are made when it becomes clear that primary research findings have been misinterpreted based on personal perceptions. Awareness of personal biases tends to occur over time, and at first, researchers might simply be unsure about emergent findings. When these uncertainties mount; data analysis decisions must be reevaluated, and emergent findings must be amended until they are firmly grounded in the data.

Validity Criteria

Saturation

Saturation, fit, and transferability are used to evaluate validity when conducting theory-generating meta-synthesis research. The criterion of saturation, which will be discussed first, is not based on the amount of raw data that has been collected. Rather, saturation is based on an awareness that emerges after many weeks to months of reflexive and rigorous data collection and analysis. Saturation is reached when investigators are confident that, despite the unlikely event that a small amount of contrary data could emerge, they would not alter the results (Corbin & Strauss, 2008; Finfgeld-Connett, 2014b).

Of note is the fact that when researchers conduct theory-generating meta-synthesis research, the data pool is finite. At any point in time, there are a fixed number of primary research reports that qualify for inclusion in the sample, and researchers are prevented from continually adding to their sample. This means that some emergent findings might remain unsaturated.

Fit

Barring saturation, emergent findings might qualify as valid if no other plausible explanation exists. This criterion of validity is known as fit, and it is particularly important when the goal is theory development, because data analysis extends beyond merely resubstantiating and relabeling existing concepts. Data analysis results in the synthesis of data across investigations so that novel phenomena can be inferentially linked to create new knowledge (Finfgeld-Connett, 2014b; Morse & Singleton, 2001). In this situation, patent saturation is not always realistic, and validity could depend on the explication of a plausible "line of argument" and the absence of any other reasonable assertion or explanation (Finfgeld-Connett, 2014b; Noblit & Hare, 1988, p. 62).

Qualitative research findings (i.e., raw data) that cannot be saturated or that do not meet the criterion of fit should be held in abeyance (Finfgeld-Connett, 2014b). This does not mean that these findings are invalid within the context of the primary study in which they were initially reported. Rather, it means that they cannot be saturated or they do not fit within the context of the current theory-generating meta-synthesis investigation. This commonly occurs when the raw data fall outside of the scope of the study.

Transferability

Transferability refers to the ability to use meta-synthesis-generated theory to guide thinking, decision-making, and action in the real world. Whether this criterion of external validity is met cannot be immediately determined by researchers. Instead, individuals in the field (e.g., clinicians) must cautiously evaluate and try out the theory (Finfgeld-Connett, 2010). Evaluating the external validity of meta-synthesis-generated theory is discussed in greater depth in Chapter 6.

Participatory action research is a promising research design for accomplishing this goal, because practitioners utilize the theory and generate insights relating to its adequacy (Genat, 2009). Over time, cumulative clinical observations (i.e., empirical evidence) could justify the need for more primary research, and an updated meta-synthesis. Updating meta-synthesis findings will be discussed in Chapter 6.

Learning Activities

Using three topically related self-selected primary qualitative research reports, complete the following activities that are involved in conducting a theory-generating meta-synthesis investigation.

1. Read, study, and highlight qualitative research findings within each research report.
2. In the margins of each report, make notations about tentative codes/categories, and format an initial coding table.
3. Extract qualitative findings and enter them into preformatted tables.
4. Based on activities 1–3 above, select a code that corresponds to findings from across studies and develop within and cross-study memos.
5. Fine-tune the cross-study memos from activity 4 and articulate a portion of a process theory.

References

Adames, S. B., & Campbell, R. (2005). Immigrant Latinas' conceptualizations of intimate partner violence. *Violence Against Women, 11*, 1341–1364. doi: 10.1177/1077801205280191

Austin, W., Gallop, R., McCay, E., Peternelj-Taylor, C., & Bayer, M. (1999). Culturally competent care for psychiatric clients who have a history of sexual abuse. *Clinical Nursing Research, 8*, 5–25. doi: 10.1177/105477389900800102

Belknap, R. A., & Sayeed, P. (2003). Te contaria mi vida: I would tell you my life, if only you would ask. *Health Care for Women International, 24*, 723–737. doi: 10.1080/07399330390227454

Berger, R. (2013). Now I see it, now I don't: Researcher's position and reflexivity in qualitative research. *Qualitative Research, 15*, 219–234. doi: 10.1177/1468794112468475

Birks, M., Chapman, Y., & Francis, K. (2008). Memoing in qualitative research: Probing data and processes. *Journal of Research in Nursing, 13,* 68–75. doi: 10.1177/1744987107081254

Buckley, C. A., & Waring, M. J. (2013). Using diagrams to support the research process: Examples from grounded theory. *Qualitative Research, 13,* 148–172. doi: 10.1177/1468794112472280

Burnette, C. E. (2013). Unraveling the web of intimate partner violence (IPV) with women from one southeastern tribe: A critical ethnography. Doctoral dissertation. Retrieved from https://ir.uiowa.edu/cgi/viewcontent.cgi?article=4577&context=etd

Corbin, J., & Strauss, A. (2008). *Basics of qualitative research 3e: Techniques and procedures for developing grounded theory.* Thousand Oaks, CA: Sage.

Davila, Y. R., & Brackley, M. H. (1999). Mexican and Mexican American women in a battered women's shelter: Barriers to condom negotiation for HIV/AIDS prevention. *Issues in Mental Health Nursing, 20,* 333–355. doi: 10.1080/016128499248529

Divin, C., Volker, D. L., & Harrison, T. (2013). Intimate partner violence in Mexican-American women with disabilities: A secondary data analysis of cross-language research. *Advances in Nursing Science, 36,* 243–257. doi: 10.1097/ANS.0b013e31829edcdb

Dovydaitis, T. (2011). *Somos hermanas del mismo dolor (We are sisters of the same pain): Intimate partner sexual violence narratives among Mexican immigrant women in Philadelphia.* (Dissertation). Philadelphia, PA: The University of Pennsylvania.

Finfgeld, D. L. (2003). Meta-synthesis: The state of the art—so far. *Qualitative Health Research, 13,* 893–904. doi: 10.1177/1049732303253462

Finfgeld-Connett, D. (2010). Generalizability and transferability of meta-synthesis research findings. *Journal of Advanced Nursing, 66,* 246–254. doi: 10.1111/j.1365-2648.2009.05250.x

Finfgeld-Connett, D. (2014a). Meta-synthesis findings: Potential versus reality. *Qualitative Health Research, 24,* 1581–1591. doi: 10.1177/1049732314548878

Finfgeld-Connett, D. (2014b). Use of content analysis to conduct knowledge-building and theory-generating qualitative systematic reviews. *Qualitative Research, 14,* 341–352. doi: 10.1177/1468794113481790

Finfgeld-Connett, D. (2015). Qualitative systematic review of intimate partner violence among Native Americans. *Issues in Mental Health Nursing, 36,* 754–760. doi: 10.3109/01612840.2015.1047072

Finfgeld-Connett, D. (2017). Intimate partner violence and its resolution among Mexican Americans. *Issues in Mental Health Nursing, 38,* 464–472. doi: 10.1080/01612840.2017.1284968

Finfgeld-Connett, D., Bloom, T. L., & Johnson, E. D. (2012). Perceived competency and resolution of homelessness among women with substance abuse problems. *Qualitative Health Research, 22,* 416–427. doi: 10.1177/1049732311421493

Finfgeld-Connett, D., & Johnson, E. D. (2013). Abused South Asian women in westernized countries and their experiences seeking help. *Issues in Mental Health Nursing, 34,* 863–873. doi: 10.3109/01612840.2013.833318

Fuchsel, C. L. M. (2012). The Catholic Church as a support for immigrant Mexican women living with domestic violence. *Social Work & Christianity, 39,* 66–87.

Fuchsel, C. L. M. (2013). Familism, sexual abuse, and domestic violence among immigrant Mexican women. *Affilia: Journal of Women & Social Work, 28,* 379–390. doi: 10.1177/0886109913503265

Fuchsel, C. L. M., Murphy, S. B., & Dufresne, R. (2012). Domestic violence, culture, and relationship dynamics among immigrant Mexican women. *Affilia: Journal of Women & Social Work, 27,* 263–274. doi: 10.1177/0886109912452403

Genat, B. (2009). Building emergent situated knowledges in participatory action research. *Action Research*, 7, 101–115. doi: 10.1177/1476750308099600

Grzywacz, J. G., Rao, P., Gentry, A., Marín, A., & Arcury, T. A. (2009). Acculturation and conflict in Mexican immigrants' intimate partnerships: The role of women's labor force participation. *Violence Against Women*, 15, 1194–1212. doi: 10.1177/1077801209345144

Ingram, M., McClelland, D. J., Martin, J., Caballero, M. F., Mayorga, M. T., & Gillespie, K. (2010). Experiences of immigrant women who self-petition under the Violence Against Women Act. *Violence Against Women*, 16, 858–880. doi: 10.1177/1077801210376889

Jones, L. (2008). The distinctive characteristics and needs of domestic violence victims in a Native American community. *Journal of Family Violence*, 23, 113–118. doi: 10.1007/s10896-007-9132-9

Kallivayalil, D. (2010). Narratives of suffering of South Asian immigrant survivors of domestic violence. *Violence Against Women*, 16, 789–811. doi: 10.1177/1077801210374209

Kim, T., Draucker, C. B., Bradway, C., Grisso, J. A., & Sommers, M. S. (2017). Somos hermanas del mismo dolor (We are sisters of the same pain): Intimate partner sexual violence narratives among Mexican immigrant women in the United States. *Violence Against Women*, 23, 623–642. doi: 10.1177/1077801216646224

Kyriakakis, S. (2014). Mexican immigrant women reaching out: The role of informal networks in the process of seeking help for intimate partner violence. *Violence Against Women*, 20, 1097–1116. doi: 10.1177/1077801214549640

Kyriakakis, S., Dawson, B. A., & Edmond, T. (2012). Mexican immigrant survivors of intimate partner abuse: Conceptualization and descriptions of abuse. *Violence and Victims*, 27, 548–562.

Lempert, L. B. (2007). Asking questions of the data: Memo writing in the grounded theory tradition. In A. Bryant & K. Charmaz (Eds.), *The Sage handbook of grounded theory* (pp. 245–264). Thousand Oaks, CA: Sage.

Liendo, N. M., Wardell, D. W., Engebretson, J., & Reininger, B. M. (2011). Victimization and revictimization among women of Mexican descent. *Journal of Obstetric, Gynecologic, & Neonatal Nursing (JOGNN)*, 40, 206–214. doi: 10.1111/j.1552-6909.2011.01230.x

Matamonasa-Bennett, A. (2013). "Until people are given the right to be human again": Voices of American Indian men on domestic violence and traditional cultural values. *American Indian Culture and Research Journal*, 37, 25–52. doi: 10.17953/aicr.37.4.e182111585n56001

Mattson, S., & Ruiz, E. (2005). Intimate partner violence in the Latino community and its effect on children. *Health Care for Women International*, 26, 523–529. doi: 10.1080/07399330590962627

Miles, M. B., & Huberman, A. M. (1994). *Qualitative data analysis* (2nd ed.). Thousand Oaks, CA: Sage.

Montalvo-Liendo, N., Wardell, D. W., Engebretson, J., & Reininger, B. M. (2009). Factors influencing disclosure of abuse by women of Mexican descent. *Journal of Nursing Scholarship*, 41, 359–367. doi: 10.1111/j.1547-5069.2009.01304.x

Morse, J. M., & Singleton, J. (2001). Exploring the technical aspects of "fit" in qualitative research. *Qualitative Health Research*, 11, 841–847. doi: 10.1177/104973201129119424

Moya, E. M., Chávez-Baray, S., & Martinez, O. (2014). Intimate partner violence and sexual health: Voices and images of Latina immigrant survivors in Southwestern United States. *Health Promotion Practice*, 15, 881–893. doi: 10.1177/1524839914532651

Noblit, G. W., & Hare, R. D. (1988). *Meta-ethnography: Synthesizing qualitative studies*. Newbury Park, CA: Sage.

Onwuegbuzie, A. J., & Leech, N. L. (2007). Validity and qualitative research: An oxymoron? *Quality & Quantity: International Journal of Methodology, 41*, 233–249. doi: 10.1007/s11135-006-9000-3

Polit, D. F., & Beck, C. T. (2017). *Nursing research: Generating and assessing evidence for nursing practice* (10th ed.). Philadelphia, PA: Wolters Kluwer.

Sandelowski, M., & Barroso, J. (2002a). Finding the findings in qualitative studies. *Journal of Nursing Scholarship, 34*, 213–219. doi: 10.1111/j.1547-5069.2002.00213.x

Sandelowski, M., & Barroso, J. (2002b). Reading qualitative studies. *International Journal of Qualitative Methods, 1*, 74–108. Retrieved from https://ejournals.library.ualberta.ca/index.php/IJQM/article/download/4615/3764

Thorne, S. (2009). The role of qualitative research within an evidence-based context: Can meta-synthesis be the answer? *International Journal of Nursing Studies, 46*, 569–575. doi: 10.1016/j.ijnurstu.2008.05.001

Thorne, S. (2017). Metasynthetic madness: What kind of monster have we created? *Qualitative Health Research, 27*, 3–12. doi: 10.1177/1049732316679370

Thorne, S., Jensen, L., Kearney, M., Noblit, G., & Sandelowski, M. (2004). Qualitative meta-synthesis: Reflections on methodological orientation and ideological agenda. *Qualitative Health Research, 14*, 1342–1365. doi: 10.1177/1049732304269888

Walker, L. E. A. (2017). *The battered woman syndrome* (4th ed.). New York, NY: Springer.

5
WRITING UP THE RESULTS

Deborah Finfgeld-Connett

The purpose of this chapter is to discuss tips for writing up theory-generating meta-synthesis research reports. Report sections will be described along with specific elements to include in each one. Problems and ways to avoid them will also be addressed.

Research Report Format

Some investigators deviate from standard reporting formats when they publish primary qualitative research reports. This results in the misplacement, obfuscation, and/or omission of key information. The same is true in regard to theory-generating meta-syntheses. To avoid these problems, scholars have developed reporting guidelines for writing up qualitative systematic reviews (e.g., France et al., 2017; Tong, Flemming, McInnes, Oliver, & Craig, 2012; Wong, Greenhalgh, Westhorp, Buckingham, & Pawson, 2013), however, none specifically relates to theory-generating meta-syntheses.

The tips for writing up theory-generating research reports that are presented in this chapter are not intended to guide research, and they should not be used to embellish investigations post hoc. Rather, they should be used to ensure that theory-generating meta-syntheses are clearly and accurately reported. This is highly important so that journal reviewers, editors, and readers are aware of the rigor involved in conducting theory-generating meta-syntheses. It is also important so that informed decisions can be made about the validity and utility of the resultant findings.

In general, researchers who conduct theory-generating meta-syntheses are urged to use the standard reporting format for peer-reviewed research articles. This format consists of the following sections, which are recognized across disciplines. Contents of each section can be adjusted to accommodate specific journal guidelines (e.g., American Psychological Association, 2010).

1. Title
2. Abstract
3. Introduction
4. Method
5. Findings
6. Discussion
7. Reference List
8. Table(s)
9. Figure(s)

The contents of each of these sections are discussed in relationship to theory-generating meta-synthesis research reports, and key points are outlined in Table 5.1.

TABLE 5.1 Research Report Sections, Elements, and Problems to Avoid

---

Title
Elements
• Topic and key contextual attributes
• Methodology

Avoid
• Unessential words
• Non-transparent language

Abstract
Elements
• Brief, clear overview of research topic, purpose, methods, findings, implications, and conclusions

Avoid
• Non-transparent language
• Undue focus on background information

Introduction
Elements
• Description of research topic, problem and its significance, purpose, and questions

Avoid
• Casting the investigation as a fishing expedition
• Lengthy descriptions of existing qualitative studies that make up the sample

---

Methods
Elements
• Overview of methodological framework
• Data collection and sampling methods
  • Strategies used to search the literature (e.g., databases, key terms, MeSH terms, cutoff dates)
  • Inclusion and exclusion criteria used to select research reports

---

(Continued)

TABLE 5.1 (Continued)

- Data analysis methods (e.g., coding, categorizing, memoing, diagramming)
- Methods used to establish validity (e.g., reflexivity, researcher triangulation)

Avoid
- Data collection templates that obscure theoretical sampling processes
- Data analysis descriptions that fail to explicate how theory (versus merely isolated concepts) was generated and validated
- Presentation of sample characteristics (e.g., purposes, methods, etc.)

Findings
Elements
- Sample characteristics (e.g., purposes, methods, etc.)
- Presentation of theory
- Figure of theory

Avoid
- Presentation of isolated concepts versus theory
- Use of outside references to support/enhance findings
- Use of quotations from primary research reports to support synthesized theory

Discussion
Elements
- Discussion of the findings in relationship to background information
- Strengths and limitations
- Ideas for further research
- Practical utility of findings
- Conclusions regarding expanded knowledge base

Avoid
- Presentation of findings
- Use of references to enhance or expand the findings
- Overstating the significance or practical utility of the findings

Reference List
Elements
- All references cited within the manuscript. Consult writing style manuals and/or journal guidelines for listing references to reports within the sample that are not cited in the manuscript.

Tables
Elements (examples)
- Literature search strategies
- Characteristics of primary research reports
- Exemplars of data coding/categorizing structure, memoing

Avoid
Lengthy tables of raw data (i.e., qualitative research findings from primary research reports)

Figure
Elements
- Fine-tuned illustration of theoretical elements and their dynamic interconnections

Avoid
- Use of uncustomized templates

Title and Abstract

Title

The title of a theory-generating meta-synthesis report should clearly identify the topic along with key contextual elements of the investigation such as gender, culture, geographic location, and so forth. In addition, authors are urged to include the methodology so that readers are aware of the type of research that was conducted.

Titles should be brief and devoid of non-essential words such as *findings from* or *a report of.* They should be professional; and catchy phrases, metaphors, and references to pop culture should be avoided. Although creative titles can spark interest, they can also make it difficult to identify articles based on keyword searches of academic (e.g., MedLine) and non-academic (e.g., Google) search engines. Clarity is also important so that readers can make a quick judgment about whether the article is of interest (Flanagan, 2017).

Abstract

Similar to report titles, a clear abstract is necessary to ensure that theory-generating meta-syntheses can be easily identified and readers can readily understand the topic. Abstracts should provide a brief but clear overview of the study topic, purpose, methods, findings, implications, and conclusions (Flanagan, 2017). Due to space restrictions, authors are urged to avoid focusing on background information. Instead, they are encouraged to concentrate on new insights that resulted from the investigation.

Introduction

The introduction to a report should include a clear description of the research topic and problem plus an explication of its significance. To avoid casting a theory-generating meta-synthesis as a fishing expedition, the research purpose and questions should be clearly outlined. This means explicitly articulating how the proposed investigation will go beyond merely exploring, understanding, or describing a topic. Instead, the research purpose and questions should be stated so that readers clearly understand what theoretical gaps were filled (Finfgeld-Connett, 2014). Given that the objective of a theory-generating meta-synthesis is to synthesize findings across primary qualitative studies, authors are urged to omit lengthy descriptions of qualitative studies that make up the meta-synthesis sample.

Methods

Qualitative meta-synthesis methods are relatively new, and theory-generating meta-synthesis methods are particularly so. For this reason, the research design and methods must be clearly described, and references should be cited.

Data Collection

To ensure transparency, literature search strategies need to be fully explained. Databases that were used to search the literature and topic-specific keywords and MeSH terms must be clearly identified. Context is important when conducting theory-generating meta-syntheses, thus, inclusion and exclusion criteria relating to age, gender, race, ethnicity, geographic location, diagnostic classification, and so forth need to be clearly documented and justified based on the purpose of the investigation and the research questions. Language filters should also be noted along with criteria that were used to include or exclude grey literature (Toews et al., 2017).

Cutoff dates that were used to search must be identified, especially when research findings from a prior point in time are no longer relevant. For example, due to advances in the treatment of hepatitis C, only recent literature relating to this topic would be appropriate for inclusion in a theory-generating meta-synthesis.

Some journals require or highly encourage authors to diagram systematic review data collection processes using templates such as the one in Figure 5.1 (Moher, Liberati, Tetzlaff, Altman, & The PRISMA Group, 2009). Although these types of linear flow diagrams are appropriate when data collection is straightforward, they can obfuscate complex sampling strategies that are used in conjunction with theoretical sampling. As such, theory-generating meta-synthesis investigators are cautioned against force-fitting their data collection strategies into preformatted templates (Thorne, 2017).

Data Extraction and Analysis

Methods that are used to identify and extract findings from research reports need to be clear, and data analysis strategies should be fully explained. Of utmost importance is the need to go beyond describing coding and categorizing strategies and explicate how memoing and diagramming were carried out to develop theory.

To inspire confidence in the findings, it is important to describe strategies that were used during data collection and analysis to ensure validity such as reflexivity and researcher triangulation. In regard to the latter, it is especially important to clarify how multiple researchers simultaneously collaborated rather than operated in a hierarchical or assembly-line manner, which could lead to biased results.

Findings

Meta-synthesis findings, including characteristics of the sample and a full explication of the resultant theory, should be presented in the findings section. Based on diagrams that were sketched throughout the data analysis process, researchers are encouraged to include a fine-tuned figure.

PRISMA 2009 Flow Diagram

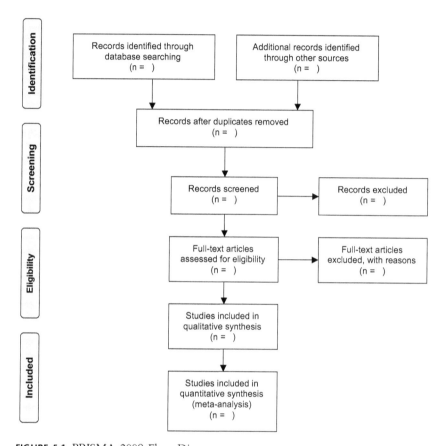

FIGURE 5.1 PRISMA 2009 Flow Diagram

The findings should be fully explanatory by themselves, and references from the literature should not be used to support or enhance the results. In addition, individual findings from primary research reports should rarely be used to bolster meta-synthesis findings, because raw un-synthesized data are generally not adequate to substantiate results that have been fully synthesized across multiple investigations. When researchers are thinking about using primary research findings in this way, they are urged to consider whether their meta-synthesis findings are fully synthesized or if they are reporting them prematurely.

Discussion

In the discussion section, the findings should be linked with background information that was presented in the introduction, and authors are urged to compare and contrast what was formally known with the resultant theoretical framework. Authors are also encouraged to clearly articulate the strengths and limitations of the study, and given these attributes, discuss ideas for further research. When practical, ways to transfer the findings to the real world should be presented. For example, the authors might explain how the resultant theory could be used to understand problems or aid in decision-making. Finally, concluding remarks should be made relating to how the findings move knowledge development forward.

It is important not to repeat the findings in the discussion section. It is also important not to bolster the results based on the literature. The overall significance and practical utility of the findings should not be overstated, and new theoretical elements should not be introduced.

Reference List

All references cited within a report should be included in the reference list. Occasionally, not all reports that comprise the sample of a theory-generating meta-synthesis are cited in a manuscript. When this occurs, writing style manuals and/or journal guidelines should be consulted to determine the appropriate format and platform (e.g., supplemental online file) for listing these references.

Tables

Tables can be used to provide information at a glance. For instance, tables are effective for clearly illustrating literature search strategies, characteristics of primary research reports, and exemplars of data coding, categorizing, and memoing. In contrast, authors are advised not to include lengthy tables of raw data (i.e., primary qualitative research findings), which have little meaning to readers.

It should be noted that there are efforts afoot among some publishers and funding agencies to encourage or even require investigators to include tables of raw data in research reports (Carpenter, 2017; Crotty, 2014; Taichman et al., 2017). When conducting meta-syntheses, this seems inappropriate for several reasons. First, when quoted findings are included in research reports, the publication process will be hindered because text recognition matching scores will be unacceptably high (e.g., iThenticate™). Second, data for meta-synthesis investigations exist in the public domain, and style guidelines for scholarly publications typically accommodate a full listing of all the references that make up a meta-synthesis sample (e.g., American Psychological Association, 2010). Third, given the context-specific research aims that drive theory-generating meta-syntheses, it is important for researchers to independently search for research reports and collect raw data from primary sources rather than appropriating data that have been extracted to answer another researcher's study-specific questions.

Figure

The goal of theory-generating meta-synthesis research is to develop a process theory, thus, a custom-made figure that clearly depicts the resultant theory is highly recommended. Fine-tuned figures help to illustrate relationships among theoretical components that are difficult to articulate, and they assist readers to understand the findings at a glance. Authors are urged to avoid using templates that have not been customized, because they are not designed to depict theory-specific components and their dynamic relationships.

Learning Activity

Based on the tips for writing up theory-generating research reports that are presented in this chapter, critique one of the articles in Appendices 2, 3, or 4.

References

American Psychological Association. (2010). *Publication manual* (6th ed.). Washington, DC: Author.

Carpenter, T. A. (2017, April 11). What constitutes peer review of data? A survey of peer review guidelines. *The Scholarly Kitchen*. Retrieved from https://scholarlykitchen. sspnet.org/2017/04/11/what-constitutes-peer-review-research-data/

Crotty, D. (2014, March 4). PLOS' bold data policy. *The Scholarly Kitchen*. Retrieved from https://scholarlykitchen.sspnet.org/2014/03/04/plos-bold-data-policy/

Finfgeld-Connett, D. (2014). Meta-synthesis findings: Potential versus reality. *Qualitative Health Research, 24*, 1581–1591. doi: 10.1177/1049732314548878

Flanagan, J. (2017). Titles and abstracts: Brevity is important. *International Journal of Nursing Knowledge, 28*, 63. doi: 10.1111/2047-3095.12174

France, E. F., Ring, N., Cunningham, M., Uny, I., Duncan, E., Roberts, R., . . . Noyes, J. (2017). *Introducing new meta-ethnography reporting guidance.* Retrieved from www. youtube.com/watch?v=58zv3PTttok&feature=player_embedded

Moher, D., Liberati, A., Tetzlaff, J., Altman, D. G., & The PRISMA Group. (2009). Preferred reporting items for systematic reviews and meta-analyses: The PRISMA statement. *PLoS Med, 6*(7), e1000097. Retrieved from http://prisma-statement.org/documents/PRISMA%202009%20flow%20diagram.doc

Taichman, D. B., Sahni, P., Pinborg, A., Peiperl, L., Laine, C., James, A., . . . Backus, J. (2017). Data sharing statements for clinical trials: A requirement of the International Committee of Medical Journal Editors. *New England Journal of Medicine, 376*(23), 2277–2279. doi: 10.1056/NEJMe1705439

Thorne, S. (2017). Metasynthetic madness: What kind of monster have we created? *Qualitative Health Research, 27*, 3–12. doi: 10.1177/1049732316679370

Toews, I., Booth, A., Berg, R. C., Lewin, S., Glenton, C., Munthe-Kaas, H. M., . . . Meerpohl, J. J. (2017). Dissemination bias in qualitative research: Conceptual considerations. *Journal of Clinical Epidemiology*. Advance online publication. doi: 10.1016/j. jclinepi.2017.04.010

Tong, A., Flemming, K., McInnes, E., Oliver, S., & Craig, J. (2012). Enhancing transparency in reporting the synthesis of qualitative research: ENTREQ. *BMC Medical Research Methodology, 12*, 181. doi: 10.1186/1471-2288-12-181

Wong, G., Greenhalgh, T., Westhorp, G., Buckingham, J., & Pawson, R. (2013). RAMESES publication standards: Realist syntheses. *Journal of Advanced Nursing, 69*, 1005–1022. doi: 10.1111/jan.12095

6

LOOKING AHEAD

Deborah Finfgeld-Connett

In this chapter, the use of meta-synthesis-generated theory is examined along with criteria for assessing whether a theory is ready for transference to practice. Comparing and contrasting findings across meta-synthesis-generated theories is discussed along with opportunities and rationale for updating them.

Use of Meta-synthesis-generated Theory

Findings from primary qualitative research investigations are sometimes viewed as impractical, because they are not intended for transference outside of the setting in which they were generated, and they are not always positioned within theory. Theory-generating meta-synthesis research fills this gap by synthesizing findings from across context-specific primary qualitative research and situating the results within generalizable process theories. These types of theories are highly important, because they enhance understanding and problem-solving, and they help to promote salutary change. Without them, change efforts are at risk of being uninformed and ineffective (Finfgeld-Connett, 2016b).

Flawed efforts to promote change are particularly worrisome in disciplines wherein enthusiasm is growing for empirically grounded practice guidelines that are largely disassociated from theory (Karnick, 2016). Within health care, algorithmic decision trees and step-by-step protocols are increasingly being used to guide diagnostic processes and interventions. Convenience aside, these formulaic guidelines are not entirely contextualized within theory, and thus, it is difficult to make fully informed decisions regarding patient care. For example, this is the case when standardized guidelines (e.g., clinical and policy guidelines for intimate partner violence and sexual violence against women [(World Health Organization, 2013)]), are used to provide care to individuals within specific cultural groups, because they are not designed to accommodate their unique needs (Thorne & Sawatzky, 2014; Thorne, 2016). In these situations, meta-synthesis-generated theories, such as those that can be found in Appendices 3 and 4, can fill this void by providing contextually based insights.

Meta-synthesis-generated Theory and Practice Guidelines

Evidence-based practice guidelines provide generalizable strategies for approaching decision-making and action; however, they do not constitute unalterable truths. Due to complex and unforeseen circumstances, practice guidelines must be adapted to efficiently and effectively provide individualized care (Hoesing, 2016; Weiringa, Engebretsen, Heggen, & Greenhalgh, 2017). Although critical thinking skills such as reflection and logical reasoning undoubtedly help practitioners analyze unanticipated situations, contextually based meta-synthesis-generated theories have the potential to optimize decision-making by providing frameworks for problem-solving (Finfgeld-Connett, 2016b).

Meta-synthesis-generated theories accommodate the insertion of context-specific information, which is based on multiple ways of knowing (e.g., empirical, esthetic, personal, and ethical [Carper, 1978]) so that decision-making can be individualized. For example, based on a meta-synthesis-generated theory relating to intimate partner violence and its resolution among Native Americans, service providers are advised to carefully assess and selectively leverage cultural strengths, such as tribal leadership customs and nonviolence norms, to successfully resolve abuse. Moreover, depending on each unique situation, providers are encouraged to assess for other underlying attributes that could enhance or inhibit the resolution process and adjust decision-making and care as necessary (see Appendix 3 [Finfgeld-Connett, 2015b]).

Transferability of Meta-synthesis-generated Theory to Practice

In terms of theory-generating meta-synthesis research, generalizability (i.e., transferability) refers to the ability to use theory outside of the context in which it was developed to enhance decision-making and action. Health-care providers are often uncertain about when this should occur. In part, this relates to the fact that components of qualitatively generated theories can be difficult to measure, and validity cannot be easily demonstrated using quantitative research methods (Finfgeld-Connett, 2016a).

In lieu of using quantitative methods to assess whether an existing meta-synthesis-generated theory is ready for transfer, scholars are urged to examine how such a theory was developed. For example, the following questions can be used to assess whether rigorous methods were used to generate the theory. Were

TABLE 6.1 Transferability of Meta-synthesis-generated Theory: Assessment Questions

Categories	Questions
Validity	• Were unbiased strategies for assembling the sample used (i.e., literature searching and selection)? • Were rigorous methods used to analyze and synthesize raw data across studies? • Were steps taken throughout the data analysis process to ensure validity (e.g., reflexivity, triangulation)? • Does the theory appear to be well grounded in findings that were extracted from primary research reports? • Do components of the theory meet the criteria for validity (i.e., saturation or fit)?
Theory	• Are the concepts and dynamic relationships that comprise the theory fully described, logical, and rationalized? • Are the contextual attributes of the theory (e.g., population, setting, culture, age group, etc.) fully articulated? • Is the theory cohesive? • Are theoretical gaps filled? • Is the theory concise, and are non-essential or extraneous elements excluded?

unbiased searching and selection strategies used to assemble the sample? Were rigorous methods used to analyze and synthesize the raw data across studies? Were steps taken throughout the data analysis process to ensure validity (e.g., reflexivity, triangulation)? Does the theory appear to be well-grounded in findings that were extracted from primary research reports? Do components of the theory meet the criteria for validity (i.e., saturation or fit) (see Table 6.1)?

Practitioners are also encouraged to assess the overall integrity of the theory. For example, are the concepts and dynamic relationships that comprise the theory fully described, logical, and rationalized? Are the contextual attributes of the theory (e.g., population, setting, culture, age group, etc.) fully articulated? Is the theory cohesive, and are theoretical gaps filled? Finally, is the theory concise, and are non-essential or extraneous elements excluded?

Once a theory is tentatively judged to be suitable for transfer, researchers are urged to work closely with clinical experts to carefully juxtapose theory with existing clinical practice guidelines and on-site circumstances (Genat, 2009; Sandelowski, 2004). Action research is recommended for this purpose wherein researchers and clinicians work collaboratively to systematically and continuously plan, act, observe, and reflect on the applicability and usefulness of theory (Cordeiro, Soares, & Rittenmeyer, 2017). This judicious evaluation process does not rule out other forms of theory testing and subsequent adaptation, however, it is consistent with the nature of the qualitative research paradigm and the complexity of clinical situations wherein assessment and adaptation are ongoing (Finfgeld-Connett, 2016a).

Comparing and Contrasting Findings Across Meta-synthesis-generated Theories

To enhance the accessibility and usefulness of contextually specific meta-synthesis-generated theories, researchers are urged to systematically and rigorously compare findings across topically related theories. For instance, findings relating to the resolution of intimate partner violence could be compared across a number of contextually specific groups, including Native Americans (Finfgeld-Connett, 2015b), older women, African Americans, Mexican Americans (Finfgeld-Connett, 2014, 2015a, 2017), and South Asian immigrants (Finfgeld-Connett & Johnson, 2013). Notably, the goal would be to systematically explicate group-specific similarities and differences so that patient-care guidelines for each group could be fine-tuned.

Updating Meta-synthesis-generated Theory

Meta-synthesis-generated theories are subject to change when new topically related findings from primary research investigations become available. Redundant validation of existing theory is not the goal of theory-generating meta-synthesis research. Thus, when planning a follow-up investigation, the research purpose and questions should clearly reflect how revised or new findings are anticipated to enhance or replace existing ones. Notably, this differs from conducting theory-generating meta-syntheses that relate to new contexts. In these situations, researchers are encouraged to conduct entirely new investigations. For example, a new context might involve a situation-specific time frame, geographic setting, or age group.

When updating or extending an existing theory, the number of research reports that will be required to achieve validity cannot be known from the outset. That said, only a few rich findings might be needed, especially if they can be synthesized with data that were held in abeyance during a previous investigation. Conversely, without any existing data, richer primary research reports will be required.

Figures are often adapted when a theory is updated, and rules vary among publishers regarding the alteration of copyrighted diagrams. Thus, authors are encouraged to check with copyright owners about revising figures for publication. Regardless of whether copyright permission is required, publication manuals (e.g., American Psychological Association, 2010) should be consulted to ensure that original sources are referenced appropriately.

Concluding Remarks

Since the late 1980s, many methods for conducting meta-syntheses have emerged, and each offers a way to move knowledge development forward. For example, aggregative methods help to detect weaknesses or gaps in our knowledge base, whereas interpretive methods help to shed new light on phenomena (Britten,

Garside, Pope, Frost, & Cooper, 2017). To maintain the integrity of different meta-synthesis methodologies, researchers are urged to remain true to their specific aims and methods. Of utmost importance is the need to understand their strengths and limitations and to utilize them with these factors in mind.

Maintaining methodological integrity does not mean blindly adhering to formulaic protocols, especially at the expense of executing creative, well-rationalized, and sound data collection and analysis methods (Thorne, 2017). Rather, it means patently explaining why a specific methodology was selected and carefully documenting the prescribed and adapted strategies that were, in fact, used (Britten et al., 2017). At the very least, careful documentation enables readers to evaluate the validity and utility of the findings. At most, clear explanations can help to prevent confusion and methodological decay.

So far, it is not entirely clear which meta-synthesis methods will stand the test of time. For now, disciplinary, governmental, and institutional research priorities and funding opportunities will influence methodological preferences. Beyond these influences, however, methods that move beyond description and toward explanation and theory development will be in demand (Britten et al., 2017; Thorne, 2017). To this end, the theory-generating meta-synthesis methodology that is described in this text is recommended.

Learning Activities

1. Contextualize the World Health Organization guidelines (http://apps.who.int/iris/bitstream/10665/85240/1/9789241548595_eng.pdf) for managing intimate partner violence based on one of the meta-synthesis-generated theories in Appendix 3 or 4.
2. Select a meta-synthesis-generated theory from Appendix 2, 3, or 4 and evaluate its transferability based on the criteria outlined in Table 6.1.
3. Identify circumstances in which it would be appropriate to update one of the meta-synthesis-generated theories in Appendix 2, 3, or 4 versus developing a new one and vice versa.

References

American Psychological Association. (2010). *Publication manual* (6th ed.). Washington, DC: Author.

Britten, N., Garside, R., Pope, C., Frost, J., & Cooper, C. (2017). Asking more of qualitative synthesis: A response to Sally Thorne. *Qualitative Health Research*. Advance online publication. doi: 10.1177/1049732317709010

Carper, B. A. (1978). Fundamental patterns of knowing in nursing. *Advances in Nursing Science, 1*(1), 13–24. doi: 10.1097/00012272-197810000-00004

Cordeiro, L., Soares, C. B., & Rittenmeyer, L. (2017). Unscrambling method and methodology in action research traditions: Theoretical conceptualization of praxis and emancipation. *Qualitative Research, 17*, 395–407. doi: 10.1177/1468794116674771

Finfgeld-Connett, D. (2014). Intimate partner abuse among older women: Qualitative systematic review. *Clinical Nursing Research, 23,* 664–683. doi: 10.1177/1054773813500301

Finfgeld-Connett, D. (2015a). Intimate partner violence and its resolution among African American women. *Global Qualitative Nursing Research, 2,* 1–8. Retrieved from http://journals.sagepub.com/doi/pdf/10.1177/2333393614565182

Finfgeld-Connett, D. (2015b). Qualitative systematic review of intimate partner violence among Native Americans. *Issues in Mental Health Nursing, 36,* 754–760. doi: 10.3109/01612840.2015.1047072

Finfgeld-Connett, D. (2016a). The future of theory-generating meta-synthesis research. *Qualitative Health Research, 26,* 291–293. doi: 10.1177/1049732315616628

Finfgeld-Connett, D. (2016b, May). *Use of meta-synthesis research to generate theory for practice.* Paper presented at 12th Annual Congress of Qualitative Inquiry, Champaign, IL.

Finfgeld-Connett, D. (2017). Intimate partner violence and its resolution among Mexican Americans. *Issues in Mental Health Nursing, 38,* 464–472. doi: 10.1080/01612840.2017.1284968

Finfgeld-Connett, D., & Johnson, E. D. (2013). Abused South Asian women in westernized countries and their experiences seeking help. *Issues in Mental Health Nursing, 34,* 863–873. doi: 10.3109/01612840.2013.833318

Genat, B. (2009). Building emergent situated knowledges in participatory action research. *Action Research, 7,* 101–115. doi: 10.1177/1476750308099600

Hoesing, H. (2016). Clinical practice guidelines: Closing the gap between theory and practice. *Joint Commission International.* Retrieved from www.elsevier.com/__data/assets/pdf_file/0007/190177/JCI-Whitepaper_cpgs-closing-the-gap.pdf

Karnick, P. M. (2016). Evidence-based practice and nursing theory. *Nursing Science Quarterly, 29,* 283–284. doi: 10.1177/0894318416661107

Sandelowski, M. (2004). Using qualitative research. *Qualitative Health Research, 14,* 1366–1386. doi: 10.1177/1049732304269672

Thorne, S. (2016). Research toward clinical wisdom. *Nursing Inquiry, 23,* 97–98. doi: 10.1111/nin.12138

Thorne, S. (2017). Metasynthetic madness: What kind of monster have we created? *Qualitative Health Research, 27,* 3–12. doi: 10.1177/1049732316679370

Thorne, S., & Sawatzky, R. (2014). Particularizing the general: Sustaining theoretical integrity in the context of an evidence-based practice agenda. *Advances in Nursing Science, 37,* 5–18. doi: 10.1097/ANS.0000000000000011

Wieringa, S., Engebretsen, E., Heggen, K., & Greenhalgh, T. (2017). Has evidence-based medicine ever been modern? A Latour-inspired understanding of a changing EBM. *Journal of Evaluation in Clinical Practice.* Advance online publication. doi: 10.1111/jep.12752

World Health Organization. (2013). *Responding to intimate partner violence and sexual violence against women: WHO clinical and policy guidelines.* Retrieved from http://apps.who.int/iris/bitstream/10665/85240/1/9789241548595_eng.pdf

GLOSSARY

Ancestral searching—reviewing the reference lists of research reports that are in a study sample to identify additional reports that might meet the inclusion criteria

Audit trail—transparent documentation of the data collection and analysis processes (e.g., literature search strategies, report selection criteria, coding, categorizing, memoing, and diagramming), which illustrates the provenance of the research findings

Bias—influences that distort data collection, sampling, and/or analysis, and thus, threaten the validity of the findings

Characteristics of primary qualitative research investigations—study attributes such as the purpose, research questions, theoretical framework, sample, and methods that provide context for understanding emergent findings

Cited reference searching—looking forward in time for relevant research reports in which key investigations are cited

Concepts—cohesive and well-defined phenomena

Data—published qualitative research findings

Data analysis—inductive development of theory based on a process of coding, categorizing, memoing, and diagramming

Data collection—process of searching for, identifying, and selecting published research reports that meet the sampling criteria, which is followed by the extraction of relevant qualitative findings for analysis

Data extraction—process of identifying qualitative research findings (i.e., raw data) from published research reports and entering them into matrices (or qualitative data analysis software) for analysis

Diagrams—figures that are developed throughout the data analysis process that depict concepts and the relationships among them

Fit—in the absence of saturation, the criterion of validity wherein a finding provides the best credible explanation (i.e., plausible line of argument)

Generalizability—criterion of external validity wherein meta-synthesis-generated theory can be used to guide thinking, decision-making, and action outside of the context in which it was generated (i.e., transferability)

Memos—explanatory notes that are developed throughout the data analysis process that help to explicate emergent concepts and the relationships among them

Meta-synthesis—broad term that encompasses many types of investigations wherein qualitative research findings are analyzed across primary research studies

Meta-synthesis-generated theory—contextually relevant, yet generalizable, process framework that consists of concepts in dynamic relationship

Peer-reviewed articles—reports that have undergone scholarly double-blind review and appear in professional journals

Primary qualitative research—research that involves the collection of raw qualitative data from personal interviews, focus groups, participant observation, diaries, etc. wherein the data are analyzed using qualitative methods

Primary qualitative research findings—fully analyzed results from primary qualitative research investigations that comprise the raw data for theory-generating meta-synthesis studies

Process theory—framework that is comprised of concepts that are in dynamic relationship

Qualitative research paradigm—research theoretical framework wherein findings are generated using inductive methods

Reference database—searchable electronic collection of reference citations (e.g., ERIC, CINAHL, PubMed, and Social Work Abstracts)

Reference management software—computer software that can be used (at a minimum) to store, organize, and retrieve complete reference citations (e.g., Endnote™, Zotero™)

Reflexivity—continuous assessment of personal perceptions throughout the research process to ensure that the research findings are not biased

Sample—collection of published research reports that meet the study inclusion criteria and that support a theory-generating meta-synthesis investigation

Saturation—criterion of validity wherein, despite the unlikely event that a small amount of contrary data could emerge, the research findings would not be altered

Search interface—electronic platform that is used to simultaneously search more than one reference database (e.g., EBSCOhost, Ovid)

Search strategy—systematic method for searching an electronic reference database or platform using key terms, authors' names, etc.

Table of contents (TOC) alerts—subscription-based email messages that include lists of early online publications as well as table of contents of recently published journal issues

Theoretical searching—iterative process of searching for research reports for inclusion in the study sample that is guided by the need to fill gaps in the emergent theory

Theoretical sampling—iterative process of selecting research reports for inclusion in the study sample that is guided by the need to fill gaps in the emergent theory

Theory—framework for understanding the world in which we live that can range from abstract to specific

Theory-generating meta-synthesis research—investigation wherein qualitative research findings from across multiple primary qualitative investigations are rigorously analyzed and synthesized to generate contextually relevant, yet generalizable, theory

Transferability—criterion of external validity wherein meta-synthesis-generated theory can be used to guide thinking, decision-making, and action outside of the context in which it was generated (i.e., generalizability)

Triangulation—confluence of factors that enhance the validity of theory-generating meta-synthesis research findings: (a) primary qualitative findings that have been generated by multiple researchers who use any number of research methods and theoretical frameworks to conduct primary qualitative research and (b) team of researchers that cooperatively and simultaneously work together to conduct theory-generating meta-synthesis research

Validity—confirmation that qualitative findings are true based on saturation or fit

APPENDIX 1

Examples of Theory-Generating Meta-synthesis Investigations

Anbari, A. B. (2015). The RN to BSN transition: A qualitative systematic review. *Global Qualitative Nursing Research, 2*, 1–11. Retrieved from http://journals.sagepub.com/doi/pdf/10.1177/2333393615614306

Finfgeld, D. L. (1999). Courage as a process of pushing beyond the struggle. *Qualitative Health Research, 9*, 803–814. doi: 10.1177/104973299129122298

Finfgeld, D. L. (2000). Self-resolution of drug and alcohol problems: A synthesis of qualitative findings. *Journal of Addictions Nursing, 12*, 65–72.

Finfgeld-Connett, D. (2009a). Management of aggression among demented or brain-injured patients. *Clinical Nursing Research, 18*, 272–287. doi: 10.1177/1054773809337577

Finfgeld-Connett, D. (2009b). Model of therapeutic and non-therapeutic responses to patient aggression. *Issues in Mental Health Nursing, 30*, 530–537. doi: 10.1080/01612840902722120

Finfgeld-Connett, D. (2010). Becoming homeless, being homeless, and resolving homelessness among women. *Issues in Mental Health Nursing, 31*, 461–469. doi: 10.3109/01612840903586404

Finfgeld-Connett, D. (2014). Intimate partner abuse among older women: Qualitative systematic review. *Clinical Nursing Research, 23*, 664–683. doi: 10.1177/1054773813500301

Finfgeld-Connett, D. (2015a). Intimate partner violence and its resolution among African American women. *Global Qualitative Nursing Research, 2*, 1–8. Retrieved from http://journals.sagepub.com/doi/pdf/10.1177/2333393614565182

Finfgeld-Connett, D. (2015b). Qualitative systematic review of intimate partner violence among Native Americans. *Issues in Mental Health Nursing, 36*, 754–760. doi: 10.3109/01612840.2015.1047072

Finfgeld-Connett, D. (2017). Intimate partner violence and its resolution among Mexican Americans. *Issues in Mental Health Nursing, 38*, 464–472. doi: 10.1080/01612840.2017.1284968

Finfgeld-Connett, D., Bloom, T. L., & Johnson, E. D. (2012). Perceived competency and resolution of homelessness among women with substance abuse problems. *Qualitative Health Research, 22*, 416–427. doi: 10.1177/1049732311421493

Finfgeld-Connett, D., & Johnson, E. D. (2011a). Substance abuse treatment for women who are under correctional supervision in the community: A systematic review of qualitative findings. *Issues in Mental Health Nursing, 32*, 640–648. doi: 10.3109/01612840.2011.584363

Finfgeld-Connett, D., & Johnson, E. D. (2011b). Therapeutic substance abuse treatment for incarcerated women. *Clinical Nursing Research, 20*, 462–481. doi: 10.1177/1054773811415844

Finfgeld-Connett, D., & Johnson, E. D. (2013). Abused South Asian women in westernized countries and their experiences seeking help. *Issues in Mental Health Nursing, 34*, 863–873. doi: 10.3109/01612840.2013.833318

Snyder, B. L. (2016). Women's experience of being interviewed about abuse: A qualitative systematic review. *Journal of Psychiatric and Mental Health Nursing, 23*, 605–613. doi: 10.1111/jpm.12353

APPENDIX 2

Perceived Competency and Resolution of Homelessness Among Women with Substance Abuse Problems

Deborah Finfgeld-Connett with Tina L. Bloom and E. Diane Johnson[1]

Despite evidence of relative prosperity in some places, homelessness remains a problem in many locales. Homelessness in Canada is estimated to range from 150,000 to 300,000 (Intraspec.ca, 2010), and in Australia the numbers are thought to hover around 105,000 (Australian Bureau of Statistics, 2008). Over the course of a year, it is estimated that 1,593,150 individuals in the United States experience homelessness. Of that number, approximately 605,397 (38%) are women residing in shelters (Substance Abuse and Mental Health Services Administration [SAMHSA], 2011). Reasons for homelessness among women include a lack of jobs and public assistance funds and a coinciding increase in poverty and home foreclosures. Other exacerbating problems among women include domestic violence, mental illness, substance abuse, and a commensurate lack of affordable treatment programs (Human Resources and Skills Development Canada [HRSDC], 2010; National Coalition for the Homeless [NCH], 2009).

Moving homeless women into stable housing can be challenging when substances of abuse such as alcohol, cocaine, and heroin are involved. Among a sample of homeless women from three Canadian cities, 82% (n = 193) were found to have at least one type of substance abuse disorder (Torchalla, Strehlau, Li, & Krausz, 2011). In the United States, it is estimated that women comprise one-fifth of the homeless who are admitted to substance abuse treatment facilities. About half of these individuals report between one and four prior treatment episodes, and 20% report five or more treatment experiences (SAMHSA, 2004). Given these recidivism rates, efforts to systematically examine and fine-tune assistance programs for homeless women with substance abuse problems are needed (O'Campo et al., 2009).

We conducted the current meta-synthesis following a prior investigation in which the process of becoming homeless, being homeless, and resolving homelessness among persistently homeless women was investigated (Finfgeld-Connett, 2010a). Based on findings from that study, it appears that becoming and being homeless are likely to involve maladaptive experiences of interpersonal abuse, neglect, and/or abandonment, all of which might be fueled by the psychic instability and/or immoral proclivities of close associates. Other contextually permeating factors include circumstantial poverty and transience, and social service system barriers. These barriers appear to extend beyond mere problems of availability and accessibility. Of particular note are intangible impediments pertaining to trust and the overall integrity of the system (Finfgeld-Connett, 2010a).

Based on findings from this same meta-synthesis (Finfgeld-Connett, 2010a), it was also concluded that resolving homelessness among a heterogeneous group of persistently homeless women involves cyclic stages. These women tend to seek assistance when crises occur, but they remain vulnerable to homelessness. It is not unusual for persistently homeless women to repeatedly engage–disengage–engage with the social service system prior to making sustained efforts to become stably housed. The cyclic nature of this process prolongs the resolution of homelessness and is attributable, at least in part, to substance abuse problems (Burlingham, Andrasik, Larimer, Marlatt, & Spigner, 2010; Finfgeld-Connett, 2010a). The specific purpose of this investigation was to articulate new insights relating to the cyclic process of resolving homelessness among adult women with substance abuse problems.

Methodology

Qualitative Meta-synthesis

Qualitative meta-synthesis, as outlined by Finfgeld-Connett (2009a, 2009b, 2010a), was used to conduct this investigation. This method was inspired by the work of Noblit and Hare (1988) and Miles and Huberman (1994), and the grounded theory approaches of Corbin and Strauss (2008) and Strauss and Corbin (1990). Qualitative meta-synthesis does not involve data aggregation or any other quantitative method. It is not a secondary analysis of raw qualitative data, nor is it a type of meta-analysis. Meta-synthesis is a methodology in which qualitative findings from existing research reports are systematically acquired and qualitatively analyzed and synthesized (Finfgeld, 2003; Finfgeld-Connett, 2010b). Qualitative meta-synthesis results in novel interpretations of qualitative findings that cannot be identified in original research reports (Thorne, Jensen, Kearney, Noblit, & Sandelowski, 2004). Within the context of meta-synthesis research, validity is not dependent on the logic of replication (Thorne et al.); rather, it is based on trustworthiness (Lincoln & Guba, 1985). One way that trustworthiness is established is through transparent data collection, extraction, and analysis methods (Finfgeld). To this end, these iterative processes, along with other ways of enhancing trustworthiness, are described in the following paragraphs.

Sample

There is some overlap (n = 23) between the reports that comprise the database for this study (N = 60) and a prior investigation (N = 45; Finfgeld-Connett, 2010a); however, with the help of an expert reference librarian (third author E. Diane Johnson), the pool of potential research reports was greatly expanded for this study. In addition, unlike the prior investigation, research reports were excluded if substance abuse issues were not addressed.

Electronic databases that were searched included Cumulative Index to Nursing and Allied Health Literature (CINAHL), ETOH Archival Database, Gender-Watch, Google Books, Ovid MedLine, ProQuest Dissertations, PsycINFO, Scopus, and Social Work Abstracts. Customized search strategies, such as the example in Table A2.1, were used to maximize the potential of each unique database and to exclude reports such as those that pertained solely to children, adolescents,

TABLE A2.1 PsycINFO Literature Search

No.	Searches	Results
1	homeless/ or homeless mentally ill/	3,878
2	(homeless$ or street people or street person$1 or living on the street$1).mp.	5,598
3	1 or 2	5,598
4	human females/ or (women or woman or female$).mp.	335,282
5	3 and 4	1,192
6	drug abuse/ or alcohol abuse/ or alcoholism/ or binge drinking/	53,587
7	drug dependency/ or drug addiction/ or heroin addiction/	16,812
8	inhalant abuse/ or glue sniffing/ or polydrug abuse/	930
9	addiction/ or drug usage/ or alcohol drinking patterns/	26,986
10	alcohol intoxication/ or acute alcohol intoxication/ or chronic alcohol intoxication/	1,909
11	social drinking/	696
12	intravenous drug usage/	2,268
13	drug abstinence/ or sobriety/	2,309
14	drug rehabilitation/ or alcohol rehabilitation/ or alcoholics anonymous/	20,789
15	methadone maintenance/	2,434
16	twelve-step programs/	407
17	drug seeking/	126
18	or/6–17	94,462
19	4 and 18 and 3	298
20	limit 19 to yr="1980-Current"	295

Note. "$" replaces characters and will find all forms of a word root; mp. = search multiple parameters (e.g., title, abstract, subject heading field) for a word and men, or those that were not conducted using qualitative methods. These tailored search strategies resulted in more than 5,500 English language citations, with unavoidable duplication across databases.

A cursory review of each citation title and abstract was conducted to further eliminate publications that were clearly not reports of qualitative research relating to homeless women. This resulted in the identification of 90 promising reports that were subsequently secured for further evaluation. Thirty of these were eliminated for one or more reasons; for example, findings relating to substance abuse could not be identified, or findings relating to women could not be separated from those pertaining to men, or findings relating strictly to homeless women could not be isolated from those associated with low income women. In total, 60 reports of qualitative research, dating from 1990 to mid-2010, comprised the sample for this investigation. This number consisted of 30 published peer-reviewed articles, seven books, and 23 theses/ dissertations.

Data Extraction, Analysis, and Synthesis

To avoid potential theoretical bias, grounded theory process concepts (e.g., antecedents, attributes, outcomes, and interrelationships among constructs; Corbin & Strauss, 2008) were the only theoretical foundations that were used for data analysis. Coding structures from a prior investigation (Finfgeld-Connett, 2010a) were not used to guide data analysis because the foci of this study and that one differ. A data collection form that was adapted from Finfgeld-Connett (2010a) was used to gather information pertaining to each study, such as aim/purpose, theoretical framework, methods, and sample. This information was used throughout the data-analysis process to provide context. When available, information relating to substance abuse treatment strategies was also gathered; however, the utility of these data was limited because they were inconsistently reported across studies.

Each research report was carefully read, and the findings were highlighted. In keeping with meta-synthesis methods, findings were limited to researcher interpretations rather than raw data such as quotations (Finfgeld, 2003; Finfgeld-Connett, 2010a). To avoid bias, all interpreted findings, regardless of how they compared with the researchers' preconceived ideas, were extracted from the original research reports and placed into data analysis matrices for coding and categorizing. Concrete and in vivo codes were initially used to ensure a firm grounding in the data. To further ensure well-grounded results, metaphorical coding was carried out in small iterative and reflexive steps. Subsequently, memos were iteratively and reflexively composed and revised to clearly articulate singular codes, explicate abstract categories, and delineate links among concepts (Finfgeld-Connett, 2010a). Memos were gradually translated into provisional lines of argument and continually evaluated against the original data to assess for truthfulness and fittingness with associated findings. This reflexive and iterative process continued until conceptual clarity was achieved and the core concept of perceived competency was fully articulated (Corbin & Strauss, 2008; Finfgeld-Connett, 2010a; Noblit & Hare, 1988).

Trustworthiness

In addition to using transparent and iterative data collection, extraction, and analysis methods, trustworthiness of the findings was enhanced in the following ways: First, instead of vetting research reports in their entirety for quality, each finding was evaluated based on its credibility and fittingness within the emergent findings (Pawson, 2006). This approach is consistent with the fact that no known valid method currently exists for establishing the overall quality of qualitative research based on written reports (Centre for Reviews and Dissemination, 2009). In the end, only those findings that lacked support within the context of the current investigation were excluded from further consideration. This is in contrast to rejecting all findings from an entire research report based on the way a study is presented or written. For example, because research reports as old as 20 years were included in the database, each finding was carefully vetted for currency. In large part, findings relating to the topic under investigation transcended time; findings that did not were excluded from further analysis. These included time-sensitive findings pertaining to treatment funding and public policy initiatives.

In terms of trustworthiness, it is notable that several forms of triangulation are inherent to meta-synthesis. This relates to the fact that findings from multiple qualitative investigations comprise the database. Forms of triangulation that were relevant to this investigation included multiple research frameworks (i.e., phenomenology, ethnography, grounded theory, and so forth), sampling methods, data analysis methods, and researchers (Finfgeld, 2003; Finfgeld-Connett, 2010b). In the case of this meta-synthesis, trustworthiness was also enhanced by the fact that the second author, Tina L. Bloom, independently reviewed codes and memos at critical junctures in the data-analysis process and provided feedback to the first author, Deborah Finfgeld-Connett. Her feedback was used to reflexively review coding, categorizing, and memoing, and to make adjustments that were congruent with the data.

Findings

Overview

The reports included in this investigation represent studies that were carried out in the United States (n = 51), Canada (n = 3), and Australia (n = 1). One was a multisite study (Canada and Scotland), and in four instances, the data collection locations were undisclosed. In light of contextual information, these four studies appear to have been carried out in the United States and Canada. The findings that comprised the sample for this meta-synthesis represent data from 1,871 homeless women. This includes data from 674 Black women, 346 White women, 252 Hispanic women, 100 women who were classified as Other, and 499 individuals whose race/ethnicity remain unknown. The study database also included findings generated from 251 staff and 74 members of the public. These numbers do not account for countless others who were included in the research process through observation and participant observation.

Moving beyond demographics, meta-synthesis findings are presented next. Based on the results of this meta-synthesis, distorted perceptions of competency, which are shaped by dysfunctional relationships and mental health problems, appear to make it challenging for women with substance abuse problems to resolve homelessness. Women with low and high levels of perceived competency grapple with challenges related to structure and control, trust, and hopelessness. Therapeutic strategies for approaching women with distorted perceptions of competency include careful assessment, caring, personalized structure and control, development of interpersonal trust, and instillation of hope. Targeted efforts to manage substance abuse and other exacerbating mental health problems are also consistent with optimal care.

Perceived Competency

Perceived competency is a concept that is inferred based on the findings of this meta-synthesis. It is the personally interpreted ability to make decisions, take action, and execute positive change in one's life. Perceived competency exists on a continuum, and is based on individual insights and interpretations. Given the enduring personal and interpersonal challenges that many homeless women face (Marcus, 2001; Padgett, Hawkins, Abrams, & Davis, 2006), they tend to present with varying levels of perceived competency. Some homeless women project a high level of perceived competency, whereas others project very little; still others lie somewhere in the middle. Supporting references are used to explicate these ideas in the following paragraphs.

Low Perceived Competency

Women with low levels of perceived competency are likely to present as chronically homeless owing to a sense of personal paralysis (Lineberger, 2009). They are apt to psychologically distance themselves from the reality of their situations (Acquaviva, 2000) and to disassociate from their mental and physical health-care needs (Enriquez, 2005; Liebow, 1993). These women tend to see themselves as unable to effect positive change, and they attribute their gridlocked status to forces beyond their control, such as the economy or the bureaucratic system (Williams, 2003). Using this mindset, fatalism tends to become a consoling way to explain a powerful and unjust world, and blame and loathing might be projected elsewhere (Acquaviva; Brink, 2001; Carroll & Trull, 2002; Lineberger;

Williams). Although adaptive in some ways, this nihilistic worldview is apt to inhibit change by obfuscating links between personal behavior and negative consequences. It might also lead to acquiescence and behavioral inertia on the part of the individual (Acquaviva; Gelberg, Browner, Lejano, & Arangua, 2004).

High Perceived Competency

Women with high levels of perceived competency also tend to present as intransigently homeless; however, their affect might be notably different than those individuals with low levels of perceived competency. Freedom and the liberty to abide by one's own value system and rules are likely to take priority over getting help in a structured setting that functions based on conventional mores and regulations (Fogel, 1997; Patterson, 2003). These women might see the treatment environment as alien, and expectations of social service providers might exceed their willingness or ability to adapt. Instead of feeling more stable and secure in a structured environment (Fogel), they tend to feel out of control, and their behavior might be disruptive (Fogel; Grella, 1994).

Homeless women with high levels of perceived competency appear to overestimate their ability to independently execute change and improve their lives outside of therapeutic environments. Based on this vantage point, they might repress or deny injustices and assume personae of strength, toughness, and autonomy (Huey & Quirouette, 2010). These women have been known to go so far as to believe that they are exceptionally lucky, skillful, strong, or manipulative. At this polarity of the continuum, homeless women might perceive that societal rules do not apply to them, which can lead to aggressive, antisocial, or criminal activities (Carroll & Trull, 2002; Gentry, 2003; Luhrmann, 2008). Consequently, they might habitually gravitate toward illegal and unsustainable activities such as drug sales and sex work (Geter, 1993; Greene, Ball, Belcher, & McAlpine, 2003; Marcus, 2001; Wheeler, 2006).

Perceived Competency at Mid-continuum

It is inferred that homeless women in the middle of the perceived competency continuum appear to have a relatively good grasp of their personal assets and limitations, and they tend to possess skills that are needed to effectively make decisions and resolve problems. These women are better equipped than those on the margins of the continuum to assertively approach social service providers, gain knowledge, build healthy supportive relationships, establish conventional daily routines, and pursue job and housing leads (Banyard, 1995; Gillette, 2001; Haydon, 2005; Sysko, 2002). They tend to be more adept at instituting creative coping strategies, and they are not as likely to rely on social services for extended periods of time (Grella, 1994). In keeping with the purpose of this meta-synthesis, these women are not the focus of this investigation.

Factors That Shape Perceived Competency

Dysfunctional Relationships

High and low perceptions of competency tend to emerge in the context of dysfunctional relationships. Many homeless women are likely to have been raised in unstable homes where there was a history of multigenerational dysfunction and loss (Trickett & Chung, 2007); it is not unusual for their parents to have been divorced, deceased, and/or substance abusers. As youth, many homeless women endured some form of neglect and physical and emotional abuse, and they might have been raised by relatives or placed in foster care at an early age (Acquaviva, 2000; Carroll & Trull, 1999, 2002; Haydon, 2005; Marcus, 2001).

As adults, homeless women frequently report that they have experienced familial abuse and/or alienation (Carroll & Trull, 2002; Lineberger, 2009; Trickett & Chung, 2007; Wheeler, 2006). Although they might seek refuge with sympathetic acquaintances and family members, these relationships are tenuous; tensions escalate over time, and eventually the women feel compelled to leave (Belcher, Greene, McAlpine, & Ball, 2001; Brink, 2001; Montgomery, McCauley, & Bailey, 2009; Williams, 2003). As a result of these types of experiences, many homeless women do not have the opportunity to develop healthy interpersonal relationships (Belcher et al.), and their social support systems are, at best, fragile (Brink; Gillette, 2001; Williams).

Among individuals with low levels of perceived competency, it is inferred that innate needs to stay interpersonally connected might sometimes override needs to ensure one's own well-being and safety (D'Amico, Barnes, Gilbert, Ryan, & Wenzel, 2009; Urbanoski, 2001). In an attempt to create mutually fulfilling relationships, these women are apt to endure a number of different types of interpersonal abuse for the short term in hopes of satisfying their need for fulfilling relationships in the long run (Haydon, 2005; Liebow, 1993; Lineberger, 2009). Among homeless women with high levels of perceived competency, it appears that they are also likely to engage in maladaptive interpersonal relationships, but they are apt to take a different form. These women might be less likely to become closely linked with men who will abuse them, but they remain highly vulnerable to ubiquitous violence and the negative consequences of activities such as serial monogamy and drug use with strangers (e.g., exposure to human immunodeficiency virus; Bourgois, Prince, & Moss, 2004; Luhrmann, 2008).

Substance Abuse and Mental Health Problems

In some instances it is difficult to determine which comes first, substance abuse or homelessness. Many times there is a family history of substance abuse or, at the very least, it can be documented at an early age (Carroll & Trull, 1999, 2002; Lineberger, 2009; Schretzman, 1999). Foregoing that, it is not unusual for substance abuse to emerge once a woman becomes homeless. Homeless women might resort to using drugs and alcohol to belong, please a sexual partner, and/ or to escape from painful realities (Brink, 2001; Enriquez, 2005; Padgett et al., 2006). No matter its inception, a self-perpetuating cycle of substance abuse and homelessness might take shape (Belcher et al., 2001). In addition, this problem might be fueled by other acute and chronic mental health conditions such as anxiety and personality, mood, and psychotic disorders (Hatton, Kleffel, Bennett, & Gaffrey, 2001; Magee & Huriaux, 2008; Sysko, 2002; Trickett & Chung, 2007).

It is inferred that substance abuse and/or mental health problems might exacerbate the misperceptions that women on each end of the perceived competency continuum experience. In severe cases, individuals might suffer from delusions of grandeur, which could significantly escalate problems related to high perceived competency. Conversely, delusional thinking could reduce a woman's already diminished sense of perceived competency and make it difficult for her to initiate positive changes (Acquaviva, 2000; Carroll & Trull, 1999, 2002; Gillette, 2001; Haydon, 2005; Marcus, 2001; Padgett et al., 2006; Trickett & Chung, 2007; Sysko, 2002; Williams, 2003; Woods-Brown, 2001).

Perceived Competency and Receptiveness to Assistance

Structure and Control Issues

The notion that many homeless women do not have well-developed adaptive skills that are needed to make long-term positive changes in their lives is supported by qualitative research findings (Carroll & Trull, 2002; Greene et al., 2003; Lineberger, 2009; Wheeler, 2006). In different ways, homeless women on each end of the perceived competency continuum appear to struggle with structure and control issues. Homeless women with low perceived competency tend to flounder and acquiesce when they are left to their own coping devices. They prefer to abdicate decision-making to others, and they are apt to flourish within supportive environments that are highly controlling and structured (Hill, 1991; Lindsey, 1997). At times, they might unobtrusively adhere to unwarranted rules and regulations simply because they fear denial of services if they do not comply (Liebow, 1993; Luhrmann, 2008; Williams, 2003).

In contrast, the same structure and control that is comforting to women with low levels of perceived competency might be interpreted as oppressive to those on the opposite end of the competency continuum. Women with high levels of perceived competency tend to deeply resent structured and controlling environments. They dislike that activities such as eating, sleeping, and parenting are subject to focused scrutiny and regulation (Flores, 2006; Fogel, 1997; Geter, 1993; Gillette, 2001; Haydon, 2005; Marcus, 2001; Urbanoski, 2001; Wheeler, 2006). They are also highly critical of the fact that, because of restrictive rules and procedures, they are unable to make personal decisions (Connolly, 2000; Urbanoski;

Wheeler). Consequently, women with elevated levels of perceived competency find it difficult to benefit from highly structured programs of assistance, and they are apt to leave prior to fully benefiting from the services that are available (Fogel; Patterson, 2003).

Trust vs. Mistrust

Due, at least in part, to a history of non-normative developmental experiences such as abuse and neglect, persistently homeless women appear to have difficulty making adaptive decisions and functioning with their own best interests in mind (Cook, 1995). One long-term repercussion includes difficulty forming adaptive interpersonal relationships with peers, significant others, and family members (Acquaviva, 2000; Carroll & Trull, 1999, 2002; Haydon, 2005; Lineberger, 2009; Marcus, 2001; Wheeler, 2006). In an effort to protect themselves from additional victimization and trauma, homeless women might have difficulty forming adaptive interpersonal connections with beneficent social service personnel (Haydon). Homeless women do not always trust that the social service system works with their best interests in mind, and they do not necessarily take advantage of the help that is available to them (Sysko, 2002). For example, homeless women do not always believe that social service providers tell them the truth (Acquaviva; Connolly, 2000), or that the justice system will protect them (Brink, 2001). They might also fear that information they share with social service providers will be used against them when child custody decisions are at stake (Hatton et al., 2001; Woods-Brown, 2001).

Because of a lack of trust, homeless women on each end of the perceived competency continuum might find it difficult to benefit from the services that are available (Sysko, 2002). Individuals with low perceived competency might not feel confident disclosing and asserting themselves, and they are likely to behave in servile and obsequious ways. These women might shape their needs to fit the services that are available rather than forthrightly seeking out assistance that is designed to specifically meet their needs (Liebow, 1993; Luhrmann, 2008; Williams, 2003). For instance, to meet their need for food and shelter, women with substance abuse problems have been known to feign domestic abuse to receive assistance at a facility that specializes in intimate partner violence. This type of behavior tends to obfuscate their real problems and hinders rehabilitation efforts (Geter, 1993; Gillette, 2001). Alternatively, women with high levels of perceived competency who lack trust might be reluctant to enter or remain in the system unless a crisis occurs. Compassionate outreach efforts might be needed to recruit them into helping environments (Apfel, 2007; Gelberg et al., 2004), and once enrolled, they might be reluctant to disclose personal information (Liebow; Gillette; Marcus, 2001). To retain them in the system, considerable effort might be needed to establish and maintain trusting relationships.

Hopelessness

Creating a new life can be challenging, even under ideal circumstances. These challenges tend to be magnified when individuals are prone to distorted perceptions of competency, and the system they must work within is rife with imperfections. For instance, complex bureaucracy is a widespread problem that can make it difficult for women with relatively few interpersonal skills to benefit from the services that are available (Brink, 2001; Hatton, 2001; Marcus, 2001; Wheeler, 2006). It is these types of problems that might heighten frustration and lead to a sense of hopelessness among women with both low and high levels of perceived competency.

Given their proclivity to develop a sense of powerlessness and to assume an inactive stance (Acquaviva, 2000; Carroll & Trull, 2002; Lineberger, 2009; Williams, 2003), it is reasonable to infer that women with low levels of perceived competency might experience a sense of hopelessness. At first, they might attach this feeling strictly to themselves. Later, they might extend this same feeling to a system that they perceive to be inefficient and ineffective. Alternatively, women with high levels of perceived competency are thought to feel hopeless when they are forced to operate within a system that they view as overly restrictive and punitive (Fogel, 1997; Liebow, 1993; Marcus, 2001; Patterson, 2003; Williams). Among the latter group, their sense of hopelessness tends to immediately transcend personal attributions and be projected onto a bureaucratic system that is perceived to be oppressive. In effect, this defense mechanism might help women with high levels of perceived competency preserve their distorted perception of competency.

Provision of Services in the Context of Distorted Perceptions of Competency

Careful Assessment

For different reasons, women on each end of the perceived competency continuum might find it difficult to optimally benefit from social services. For this reason, careful assessment is recommended (Apfel, 2007; Bridgman, 2003; Flores, 2006; Lindsey, 1997; Magee & Huriaux, 2008; Urbanoski, 2001; Williams, 2003; Woods-Brown, 2001). Having a sense of each woman's position on the perceived competency continuum is anticipated to help social service providers create and implement the most effective and efficacious assistance possible. Supplied with accurate assessment information, social service providers are better able to foresee how homeless women might present themselves, request assistance, and respond when assistance is offered. For instance, homeless women with high levels of perceived competency would be expected to present themselves as being more capable and less in need than those with low levels of perceived competency.

In addition, substance abuse problems would be anticipated to further complicate attempts to resolve homelessness (Apfel; Bridgman; Flores; Lindsey; Magee & Huriaux; Urbanoski; Williams; Woods-Brown).

Caring

Based on evidence from this investigation, it cannot be assumed that social service providers will routinely provide assistance in a caring manner. This is despite the fact that caring is perceived to be an important attribute of therapeutic assistance (Gillette, 2001; Gelberg et al., 2004; Liebow, 1993). In particular, homeless women comment on the therapeutic benefits of compassion, kindness, empathy, support, and respect. Patient, nonjudgmental communication and collaboration are valued, and the women emphasize how noncaring approaches obfuscate attempts to assist (Apfel, 2007; Gelberg et al.; Gillette; Magee & Huriaux, 2008; Urbanoski, 2001; Wenzel, D'Amico, Barnes, & Gilbert, 2009). Caring is perceived to be particularly important given that many homeless women are survivors of various forms of interpersonal trauma (Finfgeld-Connett, 2010a). It is also inferred that caring might help to diminish treatment barriers related to trust.

Development of Interpersonal Trust

Regardless of their position on the perceived competency continuum, distrust of the social service system might result in treatment barriers. Distrust is thought to stem from previous experiences in which homeless women put their trust in individuals who ultimately disappointed or failed them (Acquaviva, 2000; Carroll & Trull, 1999, 2002; Haydon, 2005; Marcus, 2001). Homeless women might also lose trust in the social service system because they were stigmatized, shamed, or blatantly mistreated by helping professionals (Acquaviva; Brink, 2001; Connolly, 2000; Gillette, 2001). In addition to building trust through caring, a holistic approach is recommended (D'Amico et al., 2009; Gelberg et al., 2004; Williams, 2003; Woods-Brown, 2001). This is not meant to imply that all services are needed or appropriate for every individual. On the contrary, each woman enters the system with her own unique needs and requires customized care and assistance (Apfel, 2007; Bridgman, 2003; Flores, 2006; Magee & Huriaux, 2008; Urbanoski, 2001; Williams; Woods-Brown). Assistance programs that are not well tailored to individual needs are inferred to promote distrust and alienation, because women might perceive that their problems are not being addressed or taken seriously.

Although homeless women build supportive relationships with social service personnel (Haydon, 2005), they cannot rely solely on these individuals for nurturance and support. For this reason, they might require assistance establishing trusting relationships with individuals outside of the helping professions. Prior to doing this, however, homeless women might need support to relinquish nonadaptive relationships (Sysko, 2002) that are characterized by interpersonal abuse and substance use (Greene et al., 2003; Schretzman, 1999; Sysko). Care providers are encouraged to foster adaptive relationships among homeless women. Researchers indicate that homeless women can build healthy supportive relationships with other homeless women that cross race, ethnicity, and sexual orientation (Haydon; Gillette, 2001). Bonding occurs based on the fact that the women share similar backgrounds and challenges, and they do not judge each other (Urbanoski, 2001). These types of supportive relationships might be helpful in terms of maintaining abstinence from alcohol and drugs (Sysko), providing comfort, and enhancing financial stability (Acquaviva, 2000).

Personalized Structure and Control

In different ways, homeless women on each end of the perceived competency continuum struggle with structure and control issues. Women with low levels of perceived competency tend to thrive in more controlled and structured environments (Liebow, 1993; Luhrmann, 2008; Williams, 2003); conversely, women with high levels of perceived competency are likely to resent these same types of milieus (Fogel, 1997; Geter, 1993; Gillette, 2001; Haydon, 2005; Marcus, 2001; Urbanoski, 2001; Wheeler, 2006). For these reasons, social service providers are encouraged to optimize assistance efforts by providing personalized structure and control (Apfel, 2007; Bridgman, 2003; Flores, 2006; Haydon, 2005; Magee & Huriaux, 2008; Urbanoski; Williams; Woods-Brown, 2001). Most homeless women appear to understand the need for at least some structure and control to live safely and amicably among others. They might even express a sense of appreciation and relief when they know that beneficent staff are present to ensure that behavioral expectations are clear and rules are judiciously applied (Bridgman; Sysko, 2002). For these individuals, fully explaining the ground rules and offering clear rationale if objections are raised might be enough to create a therapeutic milieu (Apfel). There might also be times when personalized structure and control means letting women know what type of help is available and allowing them to decide whether they will accept and actively use the services that are offered (Bridgman). This also means allowing the women to deal with the consequences of their decisions, despite the fact that those consequences might be painful (Connolly, 2000). There are, of course, instances when this type of laissez-faire approach would not be appropriate, and priorities such as safety would take precedence.

Instillation of Hope

Homeless women on both ends of the perceived competency continuum might have difficulty formulating a realistic vision of what their lives could be like. As homeless individuals, they might not see their options as plentiful, and/or they might not see one option as being significantly better than another (Grella, 1994; Montgomery et al., 2009). When making choices, they might feel as if they face the classic dilemma of choosing the lesser of two or more evils (Lineberger, 2009). For these reasons, it is important for those who work with homeless women to instill the belief that they are worthy of a better life, and to help them envision what their lives might realistically look like (Gillette, 2001; Haydon, 2005; Montgomery et al.; Sysko, 2002). To avoid perpetual disappointment and lapses into hopelessness, care providers are urged to acknowledge challenges and help homeless women envision small incremental improvements rather than the ideal (Apfel, 2007; D'Amico et al., 2009; Haydon, 2005; Liebow, 1993; Magee & Huriaux, 2008; Schretzman, 1999; Sysko).

To instill and sustain hopefulness, providers are urged to help homeless women on both ends of the perceived competency continuum develop new skill sets. Armed with new skills, individuals in each group have the potential to use them to suit their unique needs. For instance, newly acquired communication skills have the potential to enable individuals with low and high levels of perceived competency to interact more assertively rather than passively or aggressively (Banyard, 1995; Hatton et al., 2001). Other skill sets that could be honed include the art of compromise, collaborative goal setting, and decision-making (Apfel, 2007; Barkley, 1996; Connolly, 2000; D'Amico et al., 2009; Flores, 2006; Gentry, 2003; Haydon, 2005; Magee & Huriaux, 2008). Homeless women could also benefit from learning basic living skills such as how to apply for benefits, manage money, and get and retain a job (Marcus, 2001; Wheeler, 2006; Williams, 2003). Each of these is action oriented and has the potential to lead to immediate positive results and reinforcement, which might be desperately needed when individuals are experiencing hopelessness.

Another strategy that is recommended for dealing with hopelessness is spirituality. Spirituality is thought to provide homeless women with hope that their lives will improve and the supplemental nurturance that they need to see them through the process (Gillette, 2001; Greene et al., 2003; Sysko, 2002; Urbanoski, 2001). Spiritual sustenance is also associated with the intrapsychic and interpersonal support that they might require to overcome substance abuse problems (Greene et al.).

Management of Substance Abuse and Mental Health Problems

It might be difficult for persistently homeless women to take steps in a positive direction given substance abuse and mental health problems (Banyard, 1995; Grella, 1994) that might exacerbate distorted perceptions of competency. Psychotherapeutic agents might be used to treat some acute and chronic problems (Apfel, 2007). In addition, individual, substance abuse, and trauma-informed therapy are frequently recommended (Apfel; Kissman, 1999; Williams, 2003; Woods-Brown, 2001). Careful assessment is needed to know when and what type of counseling is most appropriate. For instance, counseling might be eagerly accepted in crisis situations, but individuals might be less receptive as presenting problems are resolved. This might be particularly true for individuals with high levels of perceived competency, and flexibility might be required to capture therapeutic opportunities and effectively meet the targeted needs of recipients (Urbanoski, 2001).

Discussion

Perceived Competency and Related Concepts

Many factors contribute to persistent homelessness among women. They include substance abuse, economics, and mental illness (HRSDC, 2010; NCH, 2009). Results from this investigation also point to the role that contextual factors such as long-term dysfunctional interpersonal relationships play in the emergence of distorted perceptions of competency and homelessness among women. It has been suggested that differences such as comorbid mental health problems, culture and ethnicity, domestic abuse, motherhood, and even transgender issues should be accommodated to provide optimum care to homeless women (Apfel, 2007; Bridgman, 2003; Flores, 2006; Magee & Huriaux, 2008; Urbanoski, 2001; Williams, 2003; Woods-Brown, 2001). Although this might be true, evidence from this investigation supports the notion that perceived competency could potentially transcend these differences. As such, service providers are urged to carefully determine where homeless women lie on the perceived competency continuum and accommodate their care accordingly.

Self-Efficacy

Outside of grounded theory process concepts (Corbin & Strauss, 2008), which were used to guide the research methods, no other theoretical or conceptual frameworks were employed to carry out this investigation. To examine the findings further, a systematic comparison is recommended to evaluate the similarities and differences between concepts such as self-efficacy and perceived competency. A comprehensive comparison of these two concepts is beyond the scope of this report; however, a cursory review is offered.

Like perceived competency, self-efficacy is thought to exist on a continuum ranging from low to high, and individuals on the low end of the continuum are anticipated to require considerable assistance to make adaptive changes in their lives (Bandura, 2004). Aside from this similarity, differences between the two concepts abound. Unlike perceived competency, it is proffered that the more self-efficacy individuals possess, the more likely it is that they will be able to make adaptive changes in their lives (Bandura). This is counter to findings from this investigation, which suggest that homeless women who lie in the middle of the perceived competency continuum are seen as better prepared to improve their living situations than those on the high end of the continuum.

It is noteworthy that the theorized correlation between high levels of self-efficacy and adaptive change among homeless women and women who have endured long-term abuse and trauma is not robust (Benight & Bandura, 2004; Epel, Bandura, & Zimbardo, 1999). For this reason, researchers are urged to further examine the value of concepts such as perceived competency to more fully explain the process of resolving homelessness among women.

Empowerment

Qualitative researchers do not begin research investigations devoid of information relating to their topic of interest. To manage this potential threat to trustworthiness, data analysis is conducted in a reflexive manner (Finlay, 2002). In the case of this investigation, it was tentatively hypothesized at the start that empowerment would emerge as an important strategy for helping homeless women with substance abuse problems become stably housed. In fact, empowerment was a working code well into the latter stages of data categorizing and memoing. As data analysis and synthesis progressed, however, it became clear that empowerment does not fully capture the complexity involved in such things as personalizing structure and control, making collaborative decisions, and instilling hope among women with vastly different levels of perceived competency.

Autonomy

A similar conclusion can be inferred about autonomy, a concept that was identified by O'Campo et al. (2009) in their systematic review of homeless adults with substance abuse problems. It is averred that undifferentiated promotion of autonomy among women with high levels of competency might exacerbate existing distortions. Conversely, women with low levels of perceived competency, who prefer structure, might find unbridled autonomy to be overwhelming. For these reasons, it is recommended that careful assessment and tailored promotion of autonomy be instituted to meet the unique needs of each woman.

Limitations

All meta-syntheses involve inherent limitations. Among the most serious is the researcher's distance from the original research participants. This limitation was minimized by conducting expansive sampling and carrying out careful and comprehensive data extraction. This potential limitation was also minimized by staying close to the data and using in vivo codes and transparent metaphors throughout the data analysis and synthesis processes.

In keeping with O'Campo and colleagues (2009) results from a qualitative synthesis related to homeless adults, clear guidelines for improving substance abuse outcomes could not be inferred from the data that were available for this investigation. In the case of this study, it has already been noted that data related to specific substance abuse treatment strategies were inconsistently reported across studies. In addition, although researchers were interested in substance abuse problems, immediate needs such as housing seemed to take precedence, followed closely by a keen interest in the women's overall well-being rather than merely their status as substance abusers. The latter most likely relates to the complexities involved in becoming and being homeless, and resolving homelessness vs. the more limited role that substance abuse might play as a coping mechanism (Burlingham et al., 2010).

Conclusion

Framing care for persistently homeless women within the context of perceived competency offers a new way of understanding the plight of these women and shaping interventions to assist them in establishing healthier and more stable lives. Social service providers are encouraged to carefully assess homeless women's receptiveness to assistance based on their level of perceived competency and to intervene accordingly. Suggested therapeutic strategies include development of trust, personalized structure and control, instillation of hope, and careful management of mental health problems that might exacerbate distorted perceptions of competency.

Based on the results of this investigation, social service providers are asked to reconsider blanket admonitions to enhance self-efficacy and promote empowerment and autonomy among homeless women with substance abuse problems. In addition, research is recommended to explore the similarities and differences between perceived competency and self-efficacy. Researchers are also urged to carefully examine the effectiveness of personalized structure and control vs. undifferentiated efforts to promote empowerment and autonomy when working with homeless women who are on the margins of the perceived competency continuum.

Declaration of Conflicting Interests

The authors declared no conflicts of interest with respect to the authorship and/or publication of this article.

Funding

The authors disclosed receipt of the following financial support for the research and/or authorship of this article: The project described was supported by Grant Number R21DA024749 from the National Institute on Drug Abuse. The content is solely the responsibility of the authors and does not necessarily represent the official views of the National Institutes of Health.

Note

1 Finfgeld-Connett, Deborah; Bloom, Tina L.; Johnson, E. Diane, 'Perceived Competency and Resolution of Homelessness among Women with Substance Abuse Problems', *Qualitative Health Research* 22(3), 2012, pp. 416–423. Copyright © 2012 The Authors. Reprinted by permission of SAGE Publications.

References

Acquaviva, K. D. (2000). *A qualitative study of the sexuality of women living in a homeless shelter.* (Unpublished doctoral dissertation). Philadelphia: University of Pennsylvania.

Apfel, J. (2007). *Creating surviving the streets: A trauma informed treatment guide for homeless women.* (Unpublished doctoral dissertation). San Francisco: Alliant International University.

Australian Bureau of Statistics. (2008). *Homelessness in Australia.* Retrieved from www.abs.gov.au/AUSSTATS/abs@.nsf/Latestproducts/2050.0Media%20Release12006?opendocument#

Bandura, A. (2004). Health promotion by social cognitive means. *Health Education & Behavior, 31*, 143–164. doi: 10.1177/1090198104263660

Banyard, V. L. (1995). "Taking another route": Daily survival narratives from mothers who are homeless. *American Journal of Community Psychology, 23*, 871–891. doi: 10.1007/BF02507019

Barkley, K. M. (1996). *Social change and social service: A case study of a feminist battered women's shelter.* (Unpublished doctoral dissertation). Eugene: University of Oregon.

Belcher, J. R., Greene, J. A., McAlpine, C., & Ball, K. (2001). Considering pathways into homelessness: Mothers, addictions, and trauma. *Journal of Addictions Nursing, 13*, 199–208. doi: 10.3109/10884600109052654

Benight, C. C., & Bandura, A. (2004). Social cognitive theory of post-traumatic recovery: The role of perceived self-efficacy. *Behaviour Research and Therapy, 42*, 1129–1148. doi: 10.1016/j.brat.2003.08.008

Bourgois, P., Prince, B., & Moss, A. (2004). The everyday violence of hepatitis C among young women who inject drugs in San Francisco. *Human Organization, 63*, 253–264. Retrieved from www.ncbi.nlm.nih.gov/pmc/articles/PMC1458969/pdf/nihms3845.pdf

Bridgman, R. (2003). *Safe haven: The story of a shelter for homeless women.* Toronto, ON, Canada: University of Toronto.

Brink, L. A. (2001). *"My guardian angel is working overtime": The health issues and life stories of six homeless women.* (Unpublished master's thesis). Spokane, WA: Gonzaga University.

Burlingham, B., Andrasik, M. P., Larimer, M., Marlatt, G. A., & Spigner, C. (2010). A house is not a home: A qualitative assessment of the life experiences of alcoholic homeless women. *Journal of Social Work Practice in the Addictions, 10*, 158–179. doi: 10.1080/15332561003741921

Carroll, J. J., & Trull, L. A. (1999). Homeless African American women's interpretations of child abuse as an antecedent of chemical dependence. *Early Child Development and Care, 155*, 1–16. doi: 10.1080/0030443991550101

Carroll, J. J., & Trull, L. A. (2002). Drug-dependent homeless African-American women's perspectives of life on the streets. *Journal of Ethnicity in Substance Abuse, 1*, 27–45. doi: 10.1300/J233v01n01_03

Centre for Reviews and Dissemination. (2009). *Systematic reviews: CRD's guidance for undertaking reviews in health care.* Retrieved from www.york.ac.uk/inst/crd/pdf/Systematic_Reviews.pdf

Connolly, D. R. (2000). *Homeless mothers: Face to face with women and poverty.* Minneapolis, MN: University of Minnesota.

Cook, M. A. (1995). Substance-abusing homeless mothers in treatment programs: A question of knowing. *Contemporary Drug Problems, 22,* 291–316.

Corbin, J., & Strauss, A. (2008). *Basics of qualitative research: Techniques and procedures for developing grounded theory.* Los Angeles: Sage.

D'Amico, E. J., Barnes, D., Gilbert, M. L., Ryan, G., & Wenzel, S. L. (2009). Developing a tripartite prevention program for impoverished young women transitioning to young adulthood: Addressing substance use, HIV risk, and victimization by intimate partners. *Journal of Prevention & Intervention in the Community, 37,* 112–128. doi: 10.1080/10852350902735726

Enriquez, M. P. (2005). *Health care accessibility for homeless women in Long Beach, California.* (Unpublished master's thesis). Long Beach: California State University.

Epel, E. S., Bandura, A., & Zimbardo, P. G. (1999). Escaping homelessness: The influences of self-efficacy and time perspective on coping with homelessness. *Journal of Applied Social Psychology, 29,* 575–596. doi: 10.1111/j.1559-1816.1999.tb01402.x

Finfgeld, D. L. (2003). Meta-synthesis: The state of the art—so far. *Qualitative Health Research, 13,* 893–904. doi: 10.1177/1049732303253462

Finfgeld-Connett, D. (2009a). Management of aggression among demented or brain-injured patients: A process of entering the patient's world. *Clinical Nursing Research, 18,* 272–287.

Finfgeld-Connett, D. (2009b). Model of therapeutic and nontherapeutic responses to patient aggression. *Issues in Mental Health Nursing, 30,* 530–537.

Finfgeld-Connett, D. (2010a). Becoming homeless, being homeless, and resolving homelessness among women. *Issues in Mental Health Nursing, 31,* 461–469.

Finfgeld-Connett, D. (2010b). Generalizability and transferability of meta-synthesis research findings. *Journal of Advanced Nursing, 66,* 246–254.

Finlay, L. (2002). "Outing" the researcher: The provenance, process, and practice of reflexivity. *Qualitative Health Research, 12,* 531–545. doi: 10.1177/104973202129120052

Flores, C. (2006). *Domestic violence shelters: Changes and challenges.* (Unpublished master's thesis). Carbondale: Southern Illinois University.

Fogel, S. J. (1997). Moving along: An exploratory study of homeless women with children using a transitional housing program. *Journal of Sociology and Social Welfare, 24,* 113–133.

Gelberg, L., Browner, C. H., Lejano, E., & Arangua, L. (2004). Access to women's health care: A qualitative study of barriers perceived by homeless women. *Women & Health, 40,* 87–100. doi: 10.1300/J013v40n02_06

Gentry, Q. M. (2003). *Risk in the rough: An ethnographic inquiry of how poor African-American women who smoke crack reduce their risks for HIV-infection.* (Unpublished doctoral dissertation). Atlanta: Georgia State University.

Geter, R. S. (1993). *Crack prostitution in Philadelphia: A career model.* (Unpublished doctoral dissertation). Philadelphia: University of Pennsylvania.

Gillette, S. C. (2001). *"Listen to their conversation very carefully": Homeless women talk about their health and AIDS prevention.* (Unpublished doctoral dissertation). Seattle: University of Washington.

Greene, J. A., Ball, K., Belcher, J. R., & McAlpine, C. (2003). Substance abuse, homelessness, developmental decision-making and spirituality: A women's health issue. *Journal of Social Work Practice in the Addictions, 3,* 39–56. doi: 10.1300/J160v03n01_04

Grella, C. (1994). Contrasting a shelter and day center for homeless mentally ill women: Four patterns of service use. *Community Mental Health Journal, 30,* 3–16. doi: 10.1007/BF02188871

Hatton, D. C. (2001). Homeless women's access to health services: A study of social networks and managed care in the US. *Women & Health, 33,* 167–181. doi: 10.1300/J013v33n03_10

Hatton, D. C., Kleffel, D., Bennett, S., & Gaffrey, E. A. N. (2001). Homeless women and children's access to health care: A paradox. *Journal of Community Health Nursing, 18,* 25–34. doi: 10.1207/S15327655JCHN1801_03

Haydon, E. (2005). *Homemaking/making home: The domestic lives of women living in poverty and using illicit drugs.* (Unpublished master's thesis). Toronto, ON, Canada: University of Toronto.

Hill, R. P. (1991). Homeless women, special possessions, and the meaning of "home": An ethnographic case study. *Journal of Consumer Research, 18,* 298–310.

Huey, L., & Quirouette, M. (2010). "Any girl can call the cops, no problem": The influence of gender on support for the decision to report criminal victimization within homeless communities. *British Journal of Criminology, 50,* 278–295. doi: 10.1093/bjc/azp078

Human Resources and Skills Development Canada. (2010). *The homeless partnering strategy.* Retrieved from www.hrsdc.gc.ca/eng/homelessness/index.shtml

Intraspec.ca. (2010). *Homeless in Canada.* Retrieved from http://intraspec.ca/homeless-Canada.php#PRB08-30E

Kissman, K. (1999). Time out from stress: Camp program and parenting groups for homeless mothers. *Contemporary Family Therapy, 21,* 373–384. doi: 10.1023/A:1021964416412

Liebow, E. (1993). *Tell them who I am: The lives of homeless women.* New York: Free Press.

Lincoln, Y. S., & Guba, E. G. (1985). *Naturalistic inquiry.* Newbury Park, CA: Sage.

Lindsey, E. W. (1997). The process of restabilization for mother-headed homeless families: How social workers can help. *Journal of Family Social Work, 2,* 49–72. doi: 10.1300/J039v02n03_05

Lineberger, K. A. (2009). *Unfortunate choices: "Risk in the lives of street-level sex workers and non-sex working streetwise women."* (Unpublished doctoral dissertation). Denver: University of Colorado.

Luhrmann, T. M. (2008). "The street will drive you crazy": Why homeless psychotic women in the institutional circuit in the United States often say no to offers of help. *American Journal of Psychiatry, 165,* 15–20. doi: 10.1176/appi.ajp.2007.07071166

Magee, C., & Huriaux, E. (2008). Ladies' night: Evaluating a drop-in programme for homeless marginally housed women in San Francisco's mission district. *International Journal of Drug Policy, 19,* 113–121. doi: 10.1016/j.drugpo.2007.11.009

Marcus, W. S. (2001). *Tracing bitter roots of personal violation and social displacement: A comparative phenomenological study of the life histories of homeless mothers and their dependent children.* (Unpublished doctoral dissertation). Buffalo: State University of New York.

Miles, M. B., & Huberman, A. M. (1994). *Qualitative data analysis* (2nd ed.). Thousand Oaks, CA: Sage.

Montgomery, P., McCauley, K., & Bailey, P. H. (2009). Homelessness, a state of mind? A discourse analysis. *Issues in Mental Health Nursing, 30*, 624–630. doi: 10.1080/01612840903046339

National Coalition for the Homeless. (2009). *Why are people homeless?* Retrieved from www.nationalhomeless.org/factsheets/why.html

Noblit, G. W., & Hare, R. D. (1988). *Meta-ethnography: Synthesizing qualitative studies.* Newbury Park, CA: Sage.

O'Campo, P., Kirst, M., Schaefer-McDaniel, N., Firestone, M., Scott, A., & McShane, K. (2009). Community-based services for homeless adults experiencing concurrent mental health and substance use disorders: A realist approach to synthesizing evidence. *Journal of Urban Health: Bulletin of the New York Academy of Medicine, 86*, 965–989. doi: 10.1007/s11524-009-9392-1

Padgett, D. K., Hawkins, R. L., Abrams, C., & Davis, A. (2006). In their own words: Trauma and substance abuse in the lives of formerly homeless women with serious mental illness. *Psychological Assessment, 76*, 461–467. doi: 10.1037/1040-3590.76.4.461

Patterson, W. A. (2003). *Substance abuse treatment profiling: A case study of the St. Jude Women's Recovery Center.* (Unpublished doctoral dissertation). Louisville, KY: University of Louisville.

Pawson, R. (2006). Digging for nuggets: How "bad" research can yield "good" evidence. *International Journal of Social Research Methodology, 9*, 127–142. doi: 10.1080/13645570600595314

Schretzman, M. K. (1999). *Voices of successful women: Graduates of a residential treatment program for homeless addicted women with their children.* (Unpublished doctoral dissertation). New York: The City University of New York.

Strauss, A., & Corbin, J. (1990). *Basics of qualitative research: Grounded theory procedures and techniques.* Newbury Park, CA: Sage.

Substance Abuse and Mental Health Services Administration. (2004). Characteristics of homeless female admissions to substance abuse treatment: 2002. *The DASIS Report.* Retrieved from www.oas.samhsa.gov/2k4/femHomeless/femHomeless.pdf

Substance Abuse and Mental Health Services Administration. (2011). *Current statistics on the prevalence and characteristics of people experiencing homelessness in the United States.* Department of Health and Human Services. Retrieved from http://homeless.samhsa.gov/ResourceFiles/hrc_factsheet.pdf

Sysko, H. B. (2002). *A study of homeless mothers in transition from shelter to stable housing.* (Unpublished doctoral dissertation). Pittsburgh, PA: University of Pittsburgh.

Thorne, S., Jensen, L., Kearney, M. H., Noblit, G., & Sandelowski, M. (2004). Qualitative meta-synthesis: Reflections on methodological orientation and ideological agenda. *Qualitative Health Research, 14*, 1342–1365. doi: 10.1177/1049732304269888

Torchalla, I., Strehlau, V., Li, K., & Krausz, M. (2011). Substance use and predictors of substance dependence in homeless women. *Drug and Alcohol Dependence, 118*(2–3), 173–179.

Trickett, E. M., & Chung, D. (2007). Brickbats and bouquets: Health services, community and police attitudes and the homeless experiences of women 45 years and over living in rural South Australia. *Rural Social Work and Community Practice, 12*, 5–15.

Urbanoski, K. H. (2001). *Counselling in shelters for Aboriginal women.* (Unpublished master's thesis). Calgary, AB, Canada: University of Calgary.

Wenzel, S. L., D'Amico, E. J., Barnes, D., & Gilbert, M. L. (2009). A pilot of a tripartite prevention program for homeless young women in the transition to adulthood. *Women's Health Issues, 19,* 193–201. doi: 10.1016/j.whi.2009.01.005

Wheeler, C. A. (2006). *The needs and challenges of homeless families with children as perceived by homeless-service agencies.* (Unpublished doctoral dissertation). Indianapolis: Indiana University.

Williams, J. C. (2003). *"A roof over my head": Homeless women and the shelter industry.* Boulder: University Press of Colorado.

Woods-Brown, L. Y. (2001). *Ethnographic study of homeless mentally ill persons: Single adult homeless and homeless families.* (Unpublished doctoral dissertation). Tampa: University of South Florida.

Bios

Deborah Finfgeld-Connett, PhD, PMHCNS-BC, is an associate professor at the University of Missouri Sinclair School of Nursing in Columbia, Missouri, USA.

Tina L. Bloom, RN, MPH, PhD, is an assistant professor at the University of Missouri Sinclair School of Nursing in Columbia, Missouri, USA.

E. Diane Johnson, MLS, is assistant director of information services and resources at the University of Missouri J. Otto Lottes Health Sciences Library in Columbia, Missouri, USA.

APPENDIX 3

Qualitative Systematic Review of Intimate Partner Violence Among Native Americans[1]

Deborah Finfgeld-Connett

In the United States, 5.2 million people identify as Native American, either alone or in combination with other races; and in Canada, there are around 1.5 million aboriginals. In both countries, the number of indigenous people is increasing far faster than the general population (Norris, Vines, & Hoeffel, 2012; Statistics Canada, 2011), and domestic violence is perceived to be a very serious problem (Bachman, Zaykowski, Kallmyer, Poteyeva, & Lanier, 2008; Crossland, Palmer, & Brooks, 2013; Sinha, 2013).

Exact rates of intimate partner violence (IPV) among Native Americans and Canadian aboriginals are difficult to estimate because of underreporting and methodological limitations. Despite this ambiguity, experts agree that IPV among Native Americans and Canadian aboriginals (hereafter collectively referred to as Native Americans) is more widespread than among other racially defined groups (Bachman et al., 2008; Crossland et al., 2013; Sinha, 2013). Within the US alone, 37.5% of Native American women are estimated to experience IPV in their lifetime, compared to 29.1% of Black women, 24.8% of White women, and 15.0% of Asian women (Tjaden & Thoennes, 2000).

This intractable problem has been linked to many factors, including unjust historical events, cultural attributes, oppression, and substance abuse. These links aside, breakthrough prevention and intervention strategies remain elusive and calls for greater understanding prevail. Specifically, there are persistent pleas for prevention and intervention strategies that fully take into consideration the experiences and perspectives of Native Americans (Bachman et al., 2008; Bopp, Bopp, & Lane, 2003; Crossland et al., 2013; Wahab & Olson, 2004).

To date, no known qualitative systematic review (QSR) has been conducted to comprehensively understand IPV and its resolution among Native Americans. QSR methods are ideal for bringing together isolated qualitative findings and synthesizing them to gain greater awareness of unique cultural groups. For these reasons, QSR findings have the potential to offer newly synthesized understandings relating to how IPV among Native Americans can be effectively prevented and resolved.

Specifically, the purpose of this QSR was to gain greater insight into factors that contribute to IPV among Native Americans and to more fully understand what types of services Native Americans perceive to be most acceptable and potentially helpful. Questions of interest included: (a) What historical and situational factors influence IPV among Native Americans, (b) What factors influence the effectiveness of strategies used to prevent or resolve IPV, and (c) How can helping strategies be optimized?

Methods

Methods outlined by Finfgeld–Connett (2014a, 2014b) and Finfgeld–Connett and Johnson (2013b) were used to conduct this QSR. These methods are based on grounded theory (Corbin & Strauss, 2008); thus, data analysis, interpretation, and presentation of the findings occurred with a process framework in mind.

Sample

The sample was comprised of research that pertained to the topic of IPV and Native Americans and that included qualitative findings. For the purposes of this investigation, Native Americans were defined as descendants of indigenous peoples who currently live in Canada and the US.

Keywords such as domestic violence, intimate partner violence, indigenous Americans, Native Americans, qualitative, and interview were used to search several electronic databases, including CINAHL, GenderWatch, PubMed, Social Services Abstracts, and Social Work Abstracts. Based on this search, 58 references were tentatively identified for inclusion and downloaded to EndNote. The accompanying abstracts were reviewed, and documents were excluded if they were not research reports or if they did not include qualitative findings. When this initial filtering was complete, 17 reports remained.

Upon closer examination, four documents were excluded because they did not qualify as qualitative research reports, and one was not topically relevant. Twelve reports remained, and the Scopus database was used to identify documents in which these original 12 were cited. This resulted in the identification of one additional report that met the inclusion criteria and a final count of 13 reports (i.e., 12 peer-reviewed articles and 1 dissertation) (see Table A3.1).

Data Extraction and Analysis

Each qualifying report was downloaded and saved in digital format. The reports were carefully read, and study attributes were highlighted, extracted, and organized in a table. Attributes of interest included the study purpose, theoretical framework(s), study location, sample source, sample, and methods.

To develop a data analysis framework, qualitative findings were extracted and placed into tables. Rows were organized based on report citations, and columns were arranged based on codes and categories. The body of each matrix was filled with corresponding data (i.e., qualitative research findings). Codes and categories were in flux until stable coding and categorizing was possible and saturation was achieved. As codes and categories were gradually collapsed, memos were developed to fully describe the coded/categorized data and to reflectively examine and explicate relationships among concepts.

In conjunction with memoing, a figure was developed to more clearly explicate hypothesized interconnections among concepts. Changes were continually made to the figure as relationships within the model became evident. In the end, a fully substantiated figure was developed, and key connections and interconnections among empirically grounded elements were illustrated (see Figure A3.1).

Validity

Several forms of triangulation resulted when findings from multiple primary investigations were synthesized. Researcher, theoretical, and methodological triangulation were all achieved given that the raw data (i.e., qualitative findings) that made up the database for this QSR were originally generated by many researchers using multiple theoretical frameworks (e.g., critical theory, feminist theory, phenomenology, grounded theory), and methods (e.g., data collection, analysis) (Finfgeld, 2003).

The validity of this QSR was further enhanced by using the following strategies. Raw data were held in abeyance if they could not be saturated with other

TABLE A3.1 Sampling Process

Steps	Results (+/−)	Report Tally
Searched for documents containing qualitative findings pertaining to IPV and Native Americans using the following databases:		
• CINAHL		
• GenderWatch	+58	58
• PubMed		
• Social Services Abstracts		
• Social Work Abstracts		
Culled abstracts/documents using the following exclusion criteria:		
• Non-research reports		
• Reports that lacked qualitative findings	−46	12
• Topically unrelated reports		
Searched for documents using the Scopus citation function	+1	13

findings in the study database or if they did not meet the criterion of fit. Raw data met the criterion of fit, regardless of saturation, if they helped to define hypothesized attributes or interconnections within the emergent model and if there was no other reasonable explanation for a hypothesized attribute or interconnection (Finfgeld-Connett, 2014b; Morse, 2015; Morse & Singleton, 2001).

The research reports that comprised the sample for this QSR were not evaluated, in their entirety, for quality for three reasons. First, empirically validated instruments for evaluating the quality of research reports do not exist. Second, the actual research process that is used to conduct an investigation is not always fully reflected in written reports, which can result in an incomplete or biased evaluation. Third, efforts to evaluate research reports for quality rarely result in the exclusion of reports based on quality (Finfgeld-Connett, 2014b; Sandelowski & Barroso, 2002).

Findings

Attributes of Sample Studies

The research reports that comprised the database for this QSR were generated from many disciplines including nursing, social work, family studies, criminal justice, public health, medicine, and psychology. In keeping with qualitative investigations, the purpose of each investigation was quite broad and involved exploring various aspects of IPV and its resolution among Native Americans. A number of interpretive and methodological frameworks guided the investigations, such as critical theory, feminist theory, grounded theory, enthnography, and Heideggerian hermeneutic phenomenology. In four instances, guiding frameworks were not mentioned.

Four investigations were conducted in Canada and the rest were carried out in the US. The samples were comprised of Native American women, members of the Native American community at large, health-care professionals, social service providers, and representatives of the criminal justice system. Portions of two samples appeared to overlap (Burnette, 2013; Burnette & Cannon, 2014), and data were collected primarily through personal interviews, participant observation, focus groups, and written questionnaires. Data were analyzed using a variety of coding/categorizing methods.

Overview of Qualitative Findings

Erosion of indigenous ways of living and coping appears to fuel intransigent IPV. Multifaceted IPV is entrenched and repressed within families. In crisis situations, victims are compelled to seek assistance; however, these efforts are sometimes complicated by service agencies. Attempts to resolve IPV are enhanced when agency personnel work within Native American culture to establish trust, leverage cultural strengths, and adapt services to meet specific needs.

IPV Fueled by Erosion of Indigenous Ways

Intimate partner violence among indigenous North Americans is situated within the context of history. Since the colonization of the Americas, Native people have experienced destabilizing forces such as racism, oppression, relocation, and loss (Burnette, 2013; Dylan, Regehr, & Alaggia, 2008; Jones, 2008; McKeown, Reid, & Orr, 2004; Murphy, Lemire, & Wisman, 2009). Moreover, Native societal structures and traditions have been slowly eroded and replaced with economic, educational, social, linguistic, religious, and governmental systems that are largely incompatible with indigenous ways of living and viewing the world (Burnette, 2013; Dylan et al., 2008).

As a result of these destructive forces, traditional roles and responsibilities of Native American men and women have been irreparably altered, and their customary expressions of interpersonal reverence and respect have been corrupted (Burnette, 2013; Matamonasa-Bennett, 2013). It also is believed that these same forces have led to poverty, unemployment, substance abuse, and violence in general (Dalla, Marchetti, Sechrest, & White, 2010; Jones, 2008; McKeown et al., 2004; Murphy et al., 2009).

Prior to colonization, IPV was perceived to be far less common among Native Americans due to their traditional tribal values, ethics, traditions, and the absence of alcohol. In addition, when IPV occurred, tribal elders and extended family members played a part in mediating conflicts and protecting women (Burnette, 2013; Matamonasa-Bennett, 2013).

IPV Entrenched and Repressed Within Families

IPV within Native American culture includes physical and psychological abuse, which is often characterized by patriarchal domination. It is evidenced by threats; manipulation; and physical, psychological, and financial control (Burnette, 2013; Jones, 2008). IPV often involves alcohol and drug use (Bletzer & Koss, 2004; Matamonasa-Bennett, 2013), and mutual abuse cannot be ruled out (Matamonasa-Bennett, 2013).

Multigenerational IPV is common, and abuse tends to affect all members of the family (Jones, 2008; McKeown et al., 2004). Omnipresent abuse becomes normalized over time, and tight-knit families are conditioned to survive in unstable situations (Austin, Gallop, McCay, Peternelj-Taylor, & Bayer, 1999; Burnette, 2013; Burnette & Cannon, 2014; Matamonasa-Bennett, 2013; Murphy et al., 2009).

In the home, women are likely to assume the roles and responsibilities of men; and despite the imposition of patriarchal norms, many tribal men seem to add little to the welfare of the family. Grandmothers are known to serve as the backbone of multigenerational families, and they are often the keepers of vestigial values and traditions (Burnette, 2013; Burnette & Cannon, 2014).

IPV affects Native American children in a number of ways, and merely witnessing IPV as a child can lead to long-term problems (Burnette & Cannon, 2014), including anxiety, post-traumatic stress disorder, sleep problems, low self-esteem, depression, and suicide attempts (Burnette, 2013). In the midst of IPV, parent–child loyalties and boundaries become blurred (Jones, 2008), and some children imitate abusive behaviors (Burnette, 2013; Burnette & Cannon, 2014; Dalla et al., 2010). In other instances, children try to protect their mothers (Jones, 2008).

As a result of IPV within the family, some Native American children are relocated by family services. Other children become angry and resentful and, in some instances, they run away (McKeown et al., 2004). Sexual intimacy and substance abuse tend to provide short-term solace for some adolescents, but in the end, these coping strategies are apt to promote a pattern of early pregnancy, sexually transmitted disease, educational underachievement, joblessness, IPV, and fragmented families (Burnette, 2013; Burnette & Cannon, 2014; Matamonasa-Bennett, 2013; McKeown et al., 2004).

Among Native Americans, prompt disclosure of IPV is discouraged because intact families are valued (Burnette, 2013) and close associates hope to avoid shame, guilt, and perpetrator reprisals (Austin et al., 1999; Jones, 2008; McKeown et al., 2004). Thus, despite well-developed communication networks within tribal communities (Jones, 2008), IPV is often ignored (McKeown et al., 2004).

Even though IPV is primarily perpetrated by men, many women perceive that they are at fault (Burnette, 2013). In turn, they tend to blame themselves and suppress their experiences (Jones, 2008; McKeown et al., 2004). To avoid shame, guilt, and perpetrator retribution, women remain in the home and hope for the best (Bletzer & Koss, 2004; Burnette, 2013; Jones, 2008). In time, these restrictive circumstances can provoke depression and other mental health problems, which tend to exacerbate IPV (McKeown et al., 2004). In addition, these same problems help to explain why Native Americans sometimes appear to lack motivation or the hope to overcome IPV (Jones, 2008).

To avoid total despair, Native American women nurture fragments of intra-psychic strength and courage. They learn to place physical and psychological distance between themselves and their partners while they remain in the house-hold (Murphy et al., 2009; Murphy, Risley-Curtiss, & Gerdes, 2003). Eventually, however, they experience crises, and they are forced to take action to preserve their mental and physical integrity and that of their children. Motivated by a resolve to improve their situations, women begin to take definitive steps to end IPV (Murphy et al., 2003, 2009), but barriers within service agencies tend to impede these efforts.

Service Agencies and Associated Barriers

Criminal Justice System

Many Native American women live in remote locations, and they perceive that the police respond too slowly to be helpful (Dalla et al., 2010; Jones, 2008). In addition, even when police are close, Native American women believe that the responders are indifferent or unresponsive (Dylan et al., 2008; Murphy et al., 2009). Racism is blamed for this laissez-faire attitude (Burnette, 2013; Dylan et al., 2008), but conflicts of interest also are problematic in tight-knit tribal communities where punishment and rehabilitation are difficult to mandate and enforce (Burnette, 2013).

Some Native American women find officials within the criminal justice system helpful, but many maintain that they are given inadequate or inaccurate information, and the language and protocols that are used within the judicial system are difficult to understand (Dylan et al., 2008; Murphy et al., 2009). Some women feel revictimized in court, but they also feel vindicated when their experiences are validated or when perpetrators are sentenced to jail (Dylan et al., 2008).

Social Service and Health-Care Systems

Native Americans do not always perceive that help is readily available through social service agencies or the health-care system (Austin et al., 1999; Dylan et al., 2008; Jones, 2008). Moreover, even when assistance is available, indigenous people are not eager to use these services because they fear interference, criticism, and mistreatment (Austin et al., 1999; Jones, 2008). They also fear that language barriers will obfuscate any efforts to help (Austin et al., 1999).

Many Native Americans avoid service agencies because they had been in the foster care system as children and perceive that they were victimized there; as adults, they fear that their children will be treated in the same way (Burnette, 2013). Within the mental health-care system, confidentiality is a concern (Burnette, 2013; Dalla et al., 2010), and simply rehashing stories is not perceived to be helpful (Burnette, 2013).

Work Within Native American Culture to Resolve IPV

Establish Trust

IPV within Native American communities is a complex problem that requires a holistic response from service providers who are well-informed about Native American history and culture. Without these types of insights, trust is difficult to establish and Native American women can become alienated (Austin et al., 1999; Burnette, 2013; Jones, 2008).

Cultural knowledge that is fundamental to establishing trust includes insights relating to Native American governance, including the role of tribal leaders as moderators of internal conflicts (Austin et al., 1999; Matamonasa-Bennett, 2013). Also important is the role that women and extended kin play in managing family matters, and the influence that spirituality has in the process of psychic healing. Interpersonally, service providers are urged to honor customs such as avoiding direct eye contact and respecting silence. Service providers also are encouraged to use translators, despite the challenges that a third party presents when discussing sensitive and confidential matters (Austin et al., 1999).

Additionally, it is recommended that service providers have knowledge of their own underlying perspectives and biases that could make it difficult for them to therapeutically interact with indigenous Native Americans. For example, providers are encouraged to be aware of feminist perspectives that could conflict with the type of guidance that tribal leaders might offer (Austin et al., 1999).

Leverage Cultural Strengths

Service providers are encouraged to leverage aspects of Native American culture that could promote the resolution of IPV. Although insular groups such as Native Americans are susceptible to suppressing IPV (Jones, 2008), these types of groups also have the potential to effect change from within. Approaching the problem of IPV in this way is perceived to be particularly appealing when outsiders are not fully trusted (Burnette, 2013; Jones, 2008; Matamonasa-Bennett, 2013) and language barriers could be problematic (Austin et al., 1999).

Despite the prevalence of IPV within Native American communities, indigenous people do not perceive that it is culturally appropriate or acceptable (Austin et al., 1999). In addition, Native American women and men are in favor of educating their communities about IPV (Jones, 2008), and they are open to reshaping tribal values and norms in an effort to nurture nonviolent communities (Burnette, 2013; Matamonasa-Bennett, 2013). They also are eager for tribal leaders to take an active role in managing and resolving problems within their cultural spheres of influence (Matamonasa-Bennett, 2013).

Although Native Americans value the ability to effectively function within the dominant culture (Burnette, 2013), they also support the reinvigoration of cultural traditions that have the potential to promote nonviolent environments, healthy ways of coping, autonomy, self-control, and self-esteem. Native American spiritual practices, such as prayer and sweat lodges, are perceived to be beneficial along with engaging in traditional intellectual and artistic projects. In addition, returning to Native forms of communication, such as storytelling, and leadership styles, such as talking circles, are thought to be ways of altering maladaptive power and control dynamics (Burnette, 2013; Matamonasa-Bennett, 2013; Murphy et al., 2003).

Native Americans also support the eradication of ubiquitous stressors that plague their communities and that exacerbate IPV. These include mental health problems, such as substance abuse, job and financial insecurity, illiteracy, and lack of wholesome recreational outlets (Austin et al., 1999; Burnette, 2013; Jones, 2008; Matamonasa-Bennett, 2013). In addition, they support programs to enhance public safety, nutrition, and housing, and they encourage efforts to improve environmental quality, appearance, and ambiance (Burnette, 2013).

Adapt Services

Although strengths lie within Native American communities, indigenous women often find that they need to access outside services to overcome IPV. Unfortunately, these services are difficult for many Native Americans to reach because they live in isolated rural locations. This means that timely responses from outside providers are highly important during crises. It also means that transportation to and from culturally -informed acute care and family rehabilitative services might be necessary (Burnette, 2013; Dylan et al., 2008; Jones, 2008).

Programmatically, a wide range of collaborating community services are recommended, including alcohol and drug abuse treatment programs (Jones, 2008) and parenting classes (Burnette, 2013; Jones, 2008). To enhance these services, non-Native providers are encouraged to incorporate traditional healing practices, such as talking circles, into treatment programs (Dylan et al., 2008).

In the event that non-Native service providers are unfamiliar with Native culture, they are urged to ground themselves in principles of therapeutic communication. They also are encouraged to remember that Native American women use familiar strategies to move past IPV (Austin et al., 1999). These strategies include developing a positive outlook, gaining psychological and physical distance from the perpetrator, and setting limits. Opening up, accepting oneself, and learning from mistakes also are acknowledged to be key strategies. Finally, moving forward by returning to school and, eventually, helping others can be important elements of resolving IPV (Burnette, 2013).

Providers also are reminded that, despite some similarities, important differences exist among all individuals and every IPV case should be viewed as an opportunity to gain unique insights into IPV and its resolution (Austin et al., 1999). For instance, although poverty is perceived to be pervasive among many tribes, some Native Americans have acquired financial assets by working in casinos. Thus, providers are urged to remember that money might serve as an incentive for some women to remain in abusive situations (Jones, 2008).

Discussion

Although IPV is perceived to be firmly situated within the context of Native American culture and history, many of the findings from this qualitative systematic review are similar to findings that pertain to other minority groups within Westernized countries such as South Asians (Finfgeld-Connett & Johnson, 2013a) and African Americans (Finfgeld-Connett, 2015). Similarities include cultural trauma and loss that are thought to lead to multigenerational IPV, and which is perpetuated by factors such as patriarchal norms, substance abuse, and efforts to keep flawed relationships intact. Across groups, ethnically sensitive interventions are preferred, and service providers are urged to overcome knowledge deficits and biases that serve as barriers to providing help.

Identification of generalizable evidence-based knowledge, such as the above, is fundamental to helping individuals across cultures overcome IPV. That said, situation-specific insights also are necessary to optimize helping efforts (Tanenbaum, 2014; Thorne & Sawatzky, 2014). Specifically, the process of optimizing care is thought to involve identifying context-based problems; selecting evidence-based intervention models, such as the one illustrated in Figure A3.1; modifying such models to match specific contexts; evaluating the results; and implementing additional modifications as necessary (Samuels, Schudrich, & Altschul, 2008). This type of situation-specific adaptation is illustrated in the shaded area of Figure A3.1.

Making these sorts of adjustments to theoretical models might seem obvious, however, providers appear to be moving away from model-based interventions and turning more toward evidence-based interventions that are somewhat disassociated from models/theories. In effect, it is becoming more common for intervention strategies to be based on aggregated algorithms or guidelines rather than comprehensive models/theories (Thorne & Sawatzky, 2014).

Although evidenced-based algorithms and guidelines have advantages, providers who rely solely on them in lieu of models/theories could have a rather narrow understanding of their clinical actions. Moreover, they might be reluctant to make situation-specific adjustments to their interventions because they lack a full understanding of the interventions' theoretical origins. For this reason, service providers are encouraged to have a working knowledge of evidence-based theoretical models that undergird intervention algorithms and guidelines of IPV among diverse groups (Thorne & Sawatzky, 2014).

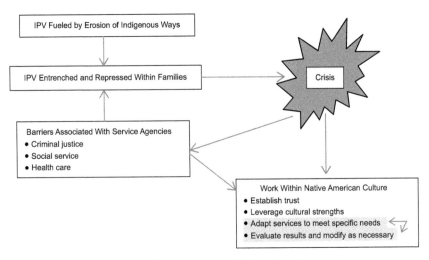

FIGURE A3.1 IPV and Its Resolution Among Native Americans

Limitations

Despite hallmarks of validity, including multiple forms of triangulation, saturation, and fit, all psychosocial models, including the one illustrated in Figure A3.1, are limited by the evidence that is available at the time and the social context in which the evidence is interpreted. In effect, all psychosocial theories are context-based and ongoing model evaluation and development is encouraged.

Conclusion

Native American families are grappling with multigenerational IPV, which is exacerbated by the loss of their culturally adaptive ways of living and coping. Strategies for overcoming IPV include diminishing barriers to services by establishing trust and leveraging cultural strengths. Providers also are encouraged to become theoretically grounded in culturally sensitive models of IPV, such as the one depicted in Figure A3.1, and to make situation-specific adaptations as needed.

Declaration of Interest: The author reports no conflicts of interest. The author alone is responsible for the content and writing of the article.

Note

1 Finfgeld-Connett, Deborah, 'Qualitative Systematic Review of Intimate Partner Violence Among Native Americans', *Issues in Mental Health Nursing* 36, 2015, pp. 754–760. Taylor and Francis, reprinted by permission of the publisher (Taylor & Francis Ltd, www.tandfonline.com).

References

Austin, W., Gallop, R., McCay, E., Peternelj-Taylor, C., & Bayer, M. (1999). Culturally competent care for psychiatric clients who have a history of sexual abuse. *Clinical Nursing Research, 8,* 5–25.

Bachman, R., Zaykowski, H., Kallmyer, R., Poteyeva, M., & Lanier, C. (2008). Violence against American Indian and Alaska Native women and the criminal justice response: What is known. *U.S. Department of Justice.* Retrieved from www.ncjrs.gov/pdffiles1/nij/grants/223691.pdf

Bletzer, K. V., & Koss, M. P. (2004). Narrative constructions of sexual violence as told by female rape survivors in three populations of the Southwestern United States: Scripts of coercion, scripts of consent. *Medical Anthropology, 23,* 113–156. doi: 10.1080/01459740490448911

Bopp, M., Bopp, J., & Lane, P. (2003). Aboriginal domestic violence in Canada. *Aboriginal Healing Foundation.* Retrieved from www.ahf.ca/downloads/domestic-violence.pdf

Burnette, C. E. (2013). *Unraveling the web of intimate partner violence (IPV) with women from one Southeastern tribe: A critical ethnography.* (Doctoral dissertation). Retrieved from http://ir.uiowa.edu/cgi/viewcontent.cgi?article=4577&context=etd

Burnette, C. E., & Cannon, C. (2014). "It will always continue unless we can change something": Consequences of intimate partner violence for indigenous women, children, and families. *European Journal of Psychotraumatology, 5*. Retrieved from www.ejpt. net/index.php/ejpt/article/download/24585/pdf_1. doi: 10.3402/ejpt.v5.24585

Corbin, J., & Strauss, A. (2008). *Basics of qualitative research: Techniques and procedures for developing grounded theory* (3rd ed.). Los Angeles, CA: Sage.

Crossland, C., Palmer, J., & Brooks, A. (2013). NIJ's program of research on violence against American Indian and Alaska Native women. *Violence Against Women, 19*, 771–790. doi: 10.1177/1077801213494706

Dalla, R., Marchetti, A., Sechrest, E., & White, J. (2010). "All the men here have the Peter Pan syndrome—they don't want to grow up": Navajo adolescent mothers' intimate partner relationships—a 15-year perspective. *Violence Against Women, 16*, 743–763. doi: 10.1177/1077801210374866

Dylan, A., Regehr, C., & Alaggia, R. (2008). And justice for all? Aboriginal victims of sexual violence. *Violence Against Women, 14*, 678–696. doi: 10.1177/1077801208317291

Finfgeld, D. L. (2003). Meta-synthesis: The state of the art—so far. *Qualitative Health Research, 13*, 893–904. doi: 10.1177/1049732303253462

Finfgeld-Connett, D. (2014a). Meta-synthesis findings: Potential versus reality. *Qualitative Health Research, 24*, 1581–1591. doi: 10.1177/1049732314548878

Finfgeld-Connett, D. (2014b). Use of content analysis to conduct knowledge-building and theory-generating qualitative systematic reviews. *Qualitative Research, 14*, 341–352. doi: 10.1177/1468794113481790

Finfgeld-Connett, D. (2015). Intimate partner violence and its resolution among African American women. *Global Qualitative Nursing Research*. Retrieved from http://gqn. sagepub.com/cgi/reprint/2/0/2333393614565182.pdf?ijkey=nm4isekj7vXn0Kd&key type=finite. doi: 10.1177/2333393614565182

Finfgeld-Connett, D., & Johnson, E. D. (2013a). Abused South Asian women in westernized countries and their experiences seeking help. *Issues in Mental Health Nursing, 34*, 863–873. doi: 10.3109/01612840.2013.833318

Finfgeld-Connett, D., & Johnson, E. D. (2013b). Literature search strategies for conducting knowledge-building and theory-generating qualitative systematic reviews. *Journal of Advanced Nursing, 69*, 194–204. doi: 10.1111/j.1365-2648.2012.06037.x

Jones, L. (2008). The distinctive characteristics and needs of domestic violence victims in a Native American community. *Journal of Family Violence, 23*, 113–118. doi: 10.1007/s10896-007-9132-9

Matamonasa-Bennett, A. (2013). "Until people are given the right to be human again": Voices of American Indian men on domestic violence and traditional cultural values. *American Indian Culture and Research Journal, 37*, 25–52.

McKeown, I., Reid, S., & Orr, P. (2004). Experiences of sexual violence and relocation in the lives of HIV infected Canadian women. *International Journal of Circumpolar Health, 63*(Suppl. 2), 399–404.

Morse, J. M. (2015). "Data were saturated . . . " *Qualitative Health Research, 25*, 587–588. doi: 10.1177/1049732315576699

Morse, J. M., & Singleton, J. (2001). Exploring the technical aspects of "fit" in qualitative research. *Qualitative Health Research, 11*, 841–847. doi: 10.1177/104973201129119424

Murphy, S. B., Lemire, L., & Wisman, M. (2009). Complex personhood as the context for intimate partner victimization: One American Indian woman's story. *American Indian & Alaska Native Mental Health Research: The Journal of the National Center, 16*,

39–59. Retrieved from www.ucdenver.edu/academics/colleges/PublicHealth/research/ centers/CAIANH/journal/Documents/Volume%2016/16(1)_Murphy_Complex_ Personhood_IPV_39-59.pdf

Murphy, S. B., Risley-Curtiss, C., & Gerdes, K. (2003). American Indian women and domestic violence: The lived experience. *Journal of Human Behavior in the Social Environment, 7,* 159–181. doi: 10.1300/J137v7n03_10

Norris, T., Vines, P. L., & Hoeffel, E. M. (2012). The American Indian and Alaska Native population: 2010 census briefs. *United States Census Bureau.* Retrieved from www. census.gov/prod/cen2010/briefs/c2010br-10.pdf

Samuels, J., Schudrich, W., & Altschul, D. (2008). *Toolkit for modifying evidence-based practices to increase cultural competence.* Orangeburg, NY: Research Foundation for Mental Health. Retrieved from http://ssrdqst.rfmh.org/cecc/sites/ssrdqst.rfmh.org.cecc/UserFiles/ ToolkitEBP.pdf

Sandelowski, M., & Barroso, J. (2002). Reading qualitative studies. *International Journal of Qualitative Methods, 1,* 74–108. Retrieved from http://ejournals.library.ualberta.ca/ index.php/IJQM/article/view/4615/3764

Sinha, M. (2013). Measuring violence against women: Statistical trends. *Statistics Canada.* Retrieved from www.statcan.gc.ca/pub/85-002-x/2013001/article/11766-eng.pdf

Statistics Canada. (2011). Aboriginal peoples in Canada: First Nations people, Métis and Inuit. *National Household Survey.* Retrieved from www12.statcan.gc.ca/nhs-enm/2011/ as-sa/99-011-x/99-011-x2011001-eng.pdf

Tanenbaum, S. J. (2014). Particularism in health care: Challenging the authority of the aggregate. *Journal of Evaluation in Clinical Practice, 20*(6), 934–941. doi: 10.1111/ jep.12249

Thorne, S., & Sawatzky, R. (2014). Particularizing the general: Sustaining theoretical integrity in the context of an evidence-based practice agenda. *Advances in Nursing Science, 37,* 5–18. doi: 10.1097/ANS.0000000000000011

Tjaden, P., & Thoennes, N. (2000). *Extent, nature, and consequences of intimate partner violence: Findings from the National Violence against Women survey.* Washington, DC: United States Department of Justice, Office of Justice Programs, National Institute of Justice. Retrieved from www.ncjrs.gov/pdffiles1/nij/181867.pdf

Wahab, S., & Olson, L. (2004). Intimate partner violence and sexual assault in Native American communities. *Trauma, Violence & Abuse, 5,* 353–366. doi: 10.1177/ 1524838004269489

APPENDIX 4

Intimate Partner Violence and Its Resolution Among Mexican Americans[1]

Deborah Finfgeld-Connett

Approximately 35.8 million residents of the United States, 11.1% of the total population, are Mexican Americans; and they make up 63.4% of the Hispanic/Latino community (United States Census Bureau [USCB], 2015). Hispanic or Latino refers to persons of Cuban, Mexican, Puerto Rican, and South or Central American origin. Hispanic or Latino also refers to persons of Spanish culture or origin regardless of race (USCB, 2011). Mexican Americans are often grouped with Hispanics/Latinos, and specific information about this subgroup can be difficult to isolate (Montalvo-Liendo, 2009; Ortiz & Telles, 2012; Rizo & Macy, 2011).

In response to demands for more information about intimate partner violence (IPV) among Hispanics/Latinos, a number of literature reviews have been conducted (e.g., Cummings, Gonzalez-Guarda, & Sandoval, 2013; Gonçalves & Matos, 2016; Klevens, 2007; O'Neal & Beckman, 2016; Rizo & Macy, 2011; Sabina, Cuevas, & Zadnik, 2015). Based on these reviews, researchers indicate that some fundamental precursors and attributes of IPV appear to be similar across Hispanics/Latinos and other cultural groups. These similarities include a history of childhood abuse, patriarchal norms, isolation, poverty, and a lack of awareness of and trust in helping services (Cummings et al., 2013; Finfgeld-Connett, 2015a, 2015b; Klevens, 2007; O'Neal & Beckman, 2016; Rizo & Macy, 2011). Conversely, context-specific aspects of IPV among Mexican Americans are somewhat obscure (Alvarez, Davidson, Fleming, & Glass, 2016; Alvarez & Fedock, 2016; Rizo & Macy, 2011).

Hispanic women in the United States are estimated to experience IPV at rates that are similar to other racial/cultural groups (~1:4); however, the mental and physical consequences of abuse appear to be disproportionately severe. This is especially true in terms of homicide and mental health problems such as suicidal ideation and suicide attempts (Alvarez & Fedock, 2016; Cummings et al., 2013; Klevens, 2007). Due to these potentially serious consequences, insights relating to IPV among Hispanic/Latino subgroups, such as Mexican Americans, are needed (Alvarez & Fedock, 2016; Klevens, 2007).

No known systematic review of strictly qualitative findings relating to IPV among Mexican Americans has been conducted. A qualitative systematic review is perceived to be particularly relevant, because qualitative research findings tend to be a rich source of context-specific information. As such, they can offer important insights into the prevention and resolution of IPV among Mexican Americans (O'Neal & Beckman, 2016). Thus, the purpose of this qualitative systematic review was to clearly articulate the process of abuse and its resolution among Mexican American women.

Methods

In general, the aim of this qualitative systematic review was to analyze and synthesize primary research findings from across study reports to generate new and more generalizable (i.e., transferable) knowledge. Generalizability is possible because findings from primary qualitative investigations, which are topically specific, yet heterogeneous, are triangulated across studies to create a new whole (Finfgeld-Connett, 2010).

Data Collection

To assess the feasibility of conducting a qualitative systematic review relating to IPV among culturally specific groups, a broad exploratory search of the English language research literature was carried out using terms such as IPV, domestic violence, partner abuse, and so forth. This search was conducted in 2011 using the following databases: CINAHL, GenderWatch, MEDLINE, PsycINFO, and Social Work Abstracts. The non–date–restricted results (N~3000) of these searches were downloaded to reference management software (i.e., EndNote™), duplicates were removed, and the titles and abstracts of each unique reference were reviewed.

Approximately 1,600 reports were excluded because they were not reports of qualitative research. The remaining qualitative research reports were grouped into context-specific categories (e.g., African Americans, Native Americans, older women, South Asians), and a substantive number of research reports (n = 34) relating to Hispanic women who had knowledge of IPV was identified. Based on closer examination, this group of reports was perceived to be too disparate to generate meaningful findings. Thus, each report was reevaluated in terms of context specificity, and 14 reports relating to adult Mexican American women living in the United States (legally or illegally) were identified.

To bring the literature search up-to-date and to ensure that a comprehensive and topically specific search had been conducted, a second non-date-restricted search of the English language literature was conducted in August and September of 2016. Academic Search Complete, CINAHL, GenderWatch, ProQuest Dissertations & Theses, PsycINFO, PubMed, Scopus, Social Services Abstracts, and Social Work Abstracts were searched. Search terms such as Mexican American, IPV, and qualitative were used and adapted to optimize the attributes of each database. As a result of these searches, four additional reports were added to the study database, which brought the total to 18.

Based on these 18 reports, ancestral and cited reference searching was conducted, but no additional reports were identified that met the inclusion criteria. Electronic table of contents alerts were set up in key research journals, such as *Violence Against Women*, and this resulted in the identification of one additional report. This article (Kim, Draucker, Bradway, Grisso, & Sommers, 2016) was based on a dissertation (Dovydaitis, 2011) that was already in the study sample. A decision was made to include both these reports in the review, because the dissertation included findings that were not reported in the peer-reviewed article, and findings in the article had been refined. At this point, data collection ceased, because no new research reports that met the study inclusion criteria could be identified, and those in the sample appeared capable of supporting the explication and validation of a context-specific qualitative systematic review.

Data Extraction, Analysis, and Synthesis

The research reports were read, and characteristics of each investigation were highlighted, extracted, and transferred to a table. The table columns were labeled as follows: reference, research purpose, theoretical framework, location, sample source, sample, and methods. This information was used to contextually situate the analysis and synthesis of the primary qualitative research findings (Table A4.1).

Qualitative findings from each primary research report were electronically copied and pasted into a formatted table. The table columns were labeled as follows: (a) references, (b) qualitative findings (i.e., raw data), and (c) within-study memos. Raw data (i.e., qualitative findings) were entered into Column B, and descriptive memos were composed in Column C to clearly distill and articulate the essence of the research findings. Memos from Column C were then iteratively grouped in accordance with a process framework (e.g., antecedents and attributes of IPV, resolution of IPV, and outcomes), and they were synthesized across studies. Synthesis involved reflexively memoing until a cohesive and well-substantiated storyline of IPV and its resolution among Mexican American women was explicated (Birks, Chapman, & Francis, 2008).

TABLE A4.1 Sample Characteristics

Reference	Purpose	Theoretical Framework	Location	Sample Source	Sample	Method
Adames and Campbell (2005)	Assess immigrant Latinas' relationships and ascertain their definition of IPV	Phenomenology	United States	Support group for women with IPV	8 women	Interviews, Thematic analysis
Belknap and Sayeed (2003)	Explore Mexican American women's perceptions of building trust when health-care providers ask them about domestic violence	Leininger's Culture Care Theory	Midwest	Spanish-speaking women receiving services from a rural domestic violence agency	7 women	Participant observation, Interviews, Thematic analysis
Davila and Brackley (1999)	Explore barriers to condom negotiation among Mexican American women who are in abusive relationships	None noted	United States	Battered women's shelter	14 women	Interviews, Content analysis
Divin, Volker, and Harrison (2013)	Explore ways in which aging Spanish-speaking women demonstrate strength in overcoming IPV	Feminist adaptation of Antonovsky's Salutogenic Theory	Texas	Flyers and promotion by community liaisons and at support groups	7 women	Secondary analysis of interview data Categorical analysis
Dovydaitis (2011)	Explore how immigrant Mexican American women describe intimate partner sexual violence	Narrative Inquiry	Philadelphia	Convenience sampling and by referral from rape crisis center	9 women	Interviews, Narrative analysis

(Continued)

TABLE A4.1 (Continued)

Reference	Purpose	Theoretical Framework	Location	Sample Source	Sample	Method
Fuchsel (2012)	Examine (a) immigrant Mexican women's understanding of the Catholic Church's position on marriage and domestic violence and (b) women's experiences of seeking help from the Church	Grounded Theory	Southwest metropolitan area	10-week, agency-based, closed support group for women	9 women	Interviews, Categorical analysis
Fuchsel (2013)	Examine relationships among childhood sexual abuse, domestic violence, and familism	Grounded Theory	Southwest metropolitan area	10-week, agency-based, closed support group for women	9 women	Interviews, Thematic analysis
Fuchsel, Murphy, and Dufresne (2012)	Examine domestic violence among immigrant Mexican women	Grounded Theory	Southwest metropolitan area	10-week, agency-based, closed support group for women	9 women	Interviews, Categorical analysis
Grzywacz, Rao, Gentry, Marín, and Arcury (2009)	Explore the relationship between intimate partner conflict and Mexican American women's entrance into the workforce	None noted	Rural western North Carolina	Community and community-based service organizations	10 women 10 men	Interviews; Theme, pattern recognition: coding, categorizing
Ingram et al. (2010)	Investigate immigration law and help-seeking among Mexican American women who experience IPV	Participatory Action Research	Two counties adjacent to Mexican border	Immigrant women who filed Violence Against Women Act self-petitions	21 women	Interviews, Content analysis

Study	Purpose	Methodology	Location	Setting	Sample	Data collection and analysis
Kelly, Lesser, Peralez-Dieckmann, and Castilla (2007)	Understand the effects of a violence awareness program on Mexican Americans	None noted	San Antonio	Community education program for Spanish-speaking immigrants	14 women; Unclarified number of program participants	Participant observation, field notes, participant journals, open-ended questions; Data coding, categorizing
Kim et al. (2016)	Explore how Mexican immigrant women describe their experiences of intimate partner sexual violence	Narrative Inquiry	Northeast	Rape crisis center	9 women	Interviews, Narrative analysis
Kyriakakis (2014)	Explore the process of seeking help for IPV among Mexican immigrant women	Grounded Theory	New York and St. Louis	Flyers and domestic violence programs in New York and health, legal, religious, and social service organizations in St. Louis	29 women; 15 service providers and community leaders	Interviews, Field notes; Categorical analysis
Kyriakakis, Dawson, and Edmond (2012)	Understand Mexican immigrant women's perceptions of IPV	Phenomenology	New York and St. Louis	Flyers and domestic violence programs in New York and health, legal, religious, and social service organizations in St. Louis	29 women	Interviews, Categorical analysis and memoing
Liendo, Wardell, Engebretson, and Reininger (2011)	Understand the experiences of Mexican American women who live with intimate partner abuse	None noted	Community adjacent to Mexican border	Shelter and outreach agency	26 women	Interviews, Descriptive qualitative approach

(Continued)

TABLE A4.1 (Continued)

Reference	Purpose	Theoretical Framework	Location	Sample Source	Sample	Method
Mattson and Ruiz (2005)	Identify the role that Mexican culture plays in IPV	None noted	United States	Men: • Clinic that serves immigrant populations • Radio and newspaper ads in Spanish language media • Head Start program Women: • Domestic violence shelters • Homeless shelter • Head Start program	N = unclarified	Focus groups, Thematic analysis
Montalvo-Liendo, Wardell, Engebretson, and Reininger (2009)	Describe factors that influence disclosure of abuse by women of Mexican descent	Grounded Theory	Community adjacent to Mexican border	Shelter and outreach agency	26 women	Interviews, Grounded Theory
Moya, Chávez-Baray, and Martinez (2014)	Assess the relationship between intimate partner violence and sexual health among Mexican immigrants	Community-based Participatory Approach	El Paso	Two community-based agencies serving Latinas affected by IPV	22 women	Photovoice, Thematic analysis
Salcido and Adelman (2004)	Explore the lives of battered Mexican American women	Ethnography	Phoenix metropolitan area	Domestic violence workshops at a community center and an adult school education program	10 women	Interviews

Validity

Validity was ensured by conducting a thorough search of the research literature and collecting all known qualitative research reports relating to the topic under investigation. Research reports were not evaluated for quality, because doing so rarely results in the exclusion of reports. Moreover, the validity of criteria for evaluating reports is unknown. Instead, raw data (i.e., qualitative research findings) were evaluated based on fit and on whether they helped saturate findings that were synthesized across studies. Saturation was reached when the synthesized findings would not have been altered even in the event that a small amount of contrary data emerged. Validity was also ensured based on triangulation, which was achieved by reflexively analyzing and synthesizing qualitative research findings from across multiple investigations that were conducted by many investigators who used a number of research frameworks (e.g., grounded theory) and data collection and analysis methods (Finfgeld-Connett, 2014; Sandelowski & Barroso, 2002; Thorne, 2009).

Findings

Sample Characteristics

Nineteen qualitative research reports comprised the sample for this systematic review. In a number of instances, two to three research reports were generated from a single sample, leaving 14 unique samples across 19 research reports. In keeping with qualitative research, sample sizes were small, ranging from seven to 29 participants. Excluding two reports wherein sample size was not specified, 196 unique respondents participated in the primary research studies that comprised the sample for this investigation.

In general, the purpose of these investigations was to explore IPV and its resolution among Mexican American women. The studies were conducted in urban and rural locations throughout the Northeast, Midwest, Southeast, and Southwest United States. Participants were recruited from agencies that provide help to victims of IPV, including support groups, domestic violence agencies, shelters, and rape crisis centers. Respondents were also recruited from an immigrant service agency and programs for Spanish-speaking women.

Many research frameworks were used to conduct the studies, including culture care theory, ethnography, feminist adaptation of salutogenic theory, grounded theory, narrative inquiry, participatory action research, and phenomenology. In five instances, a research theoretical framework was not mentioned. Data were primarily collected through interviews; however, they were also collected through field notes, focus groups, images, journals, and participatory observation. Narrative, categorical, and thematic analysis methods were used to analyze the data. The qualitative results of this systematic review are presented next and in Figure A4.1.

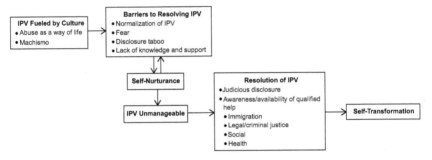

FIGURE A4.1 IPV and Its Resolution Among Mexican Americans

IPV Fueled by Culture

Abuse as a Way of Life

It is not uncommon for abused Mexican American women to be repeatedly mistreated by family members and friends (Adames & Campbell, 2005; Davila & Brackley, 1999; Divin et al., 2013; Fuchsel, 2013; Kim et al., 2016; Liendo et al., 2011; Mattson & Ruiz, 2005; Montalvo-Liendo et al., 2009). As a result, they are apt to leave their nuclear families early, marry, and reexperience abuse with their intimate partners. Among women who are sexually abused by non-family members, cultural mores tend to obligate them to marry the perpetrator, and the cycle of abuse continues (Divin et al., 2013; Fuchsel et al., 2012; Kim et al., 2016).

Machismo

IPV is fueled by machismo, wherein men are expected to be paternalistic, domineering, and controlling (Adames & Campbell, 2005; Davila & Brackley, 1999; Grzywacz et al., 2009; Kyriakakis et al., 2012; Mattson & Ruiz, 2005). Conversely, women are expected to be subservient and to take care of the home and family (Grzywacz et al., 2009; Kyriakakis et al., 2012; Montalvo-Liendo et al., 2009; Moya et al., 2014).

When Mexican American women enter the United States, they are often forced to seek employment outside of the home to make ends meet (Grzywacz et al., 2009; Kyriakakis et al., 2012). This upsets the traditional family structure, and Mexican American men are forced to share their roles as family breadwinners and decision makers. Mexican American men must adjust to losing power and control, and they must adapt to receiving less time and attention from their wives (Adames & Campbell, 2005; Grzywacz et al., 2009). To ease their distress, some Mexican American men resort to extra-marital affairs and/or alcohol and drug abuse (Adames & Campbell, 2005; Fuchsel et al., 2012; Kyriakakis et al., 2012; Mattson & Ruiz, 2005).

Types of IPV and Its Effects

Mexican American women are vulnerable to physical, sexual, verbal, psychological, and financial malevolence (Adames & Campbell, 2005; Davila & Brackley, 1999; Divin et al., 2013; Kyriakakis et al., 2012; Moya et al., 2014), all of which tends to result in diminished health. Mental and physical health problems include shame, humiliation, fear, hopelessness, loneliness, lack of interest, low self-esteem and self-confidence, clinical depression, sexually transmitted diseases, and unplanned pregnancies (Adames & Campbell, 2005; Davila & Brackley, 1999; Fuchsel et al., 2012; Kyriakakis et al., 2012; Moya et al., 2014).

Barriers to Resolving IPV

Normalization

Due to cultural norms that discourage divorce (Adames & Campbell, 2005; Fuchsel et al., 2012; Mattson & Ruiz, 2005), Mexican American women are apt to deny and normalize abuse (Liendo et al., 2011; Moya et al., 2014). They tend to feel ambivalent about their partners, and they vacillate between loving and fearing them (Montalvo-Liendo et al., 2009). Some women leave their homes for short periods, and they return when they feel that the threat has diminished (Fuchsel et al., 2012).

Fear

At first, Mexican American women avoid taking definitive action to resolve IPV, because they fear that they will find themselves in unfamiliar circumstances and will be unable to fluently speak the language. They are afraid of becoming impoverished (Fuchsel et al., 2012; Kyriakakis, 2014; Kyriakakis et al., 2012; Mattson & Ruiz, 2005), and some fear that they will have to resort to fraud or the sex trade industry to survive (Salcido & Adelman, 2004). Mexican American women are also reluctant to separate from their partners, because they are afraid that their immigration status will be threatened and/or they will lose custody of their children (Ingram et al., 2010; Montalvo-Liendo et al., 2009; Moya et al., 2014).

Disclosure Taboo

Disclosure of IPV is complicated by the fact that within Mexican culture, sharing problems outside of the family is taboo, and speaking out could lead to shame, guilt, and/or more abuse (Fuchsel, 2013; Fuchsel et al., 2012; Kyriakakis, 2014; Salcido & Adelman, 2004). To complicate matters, close and extended family members are not always reliable confidants, because they could be involved in perpetrating abuse (Kim et al., 2016; Kyriakakis, 2014; Liendo et al., 2011; Montalvo-Liendo et al., 2009). Sometimes, older children try to help (Kyriakakis,

2014), but they might also enact the same type of abuse that they have witnessed and/or endured for years (Liendo et al., 2011). Finally, well-meaning, but uninformed, family members could make matters worse by encouraging victims to work things out (Kyriakakis, 2014).

Lack of Knowledge and Support

Mexican American women are usually uninformed about social services and legal resources (Adames & Campbell, 2005; Ingram et al., 2010; Moya et al., 2014), and they do not feel confident that the criminal justice system will work in their best interest (Ingram et al., 2010; Liendo et al., 2011; Mattson & Ruiz, 2005). Within the health-care system, providers are often reluctant to broach the topic of IPV, even when suspicious injuries exist (Belknap & Sayeed, 2003; Montalvo-Liendo et al., 2009). Finally, responses from Catholic and non-Catholic pastoral staff can range from supportive to unsupportive (Fuchsel, 2012).

Self-Nurturance

Barriers to resolving IPV explain why many Mexican American women remain in abusive relationships for lengthy periods of time during which they consistently work to protect themselves and manage stress. Some find meaning and a will to live through their children. Others nurture themselves by focusing on spirituality, nature, gardening, pets, and so forth (Divin et al., 2013; Dovydaitis, 2011; Fuchsel et al., 2012). Before taking definitive action, some women note that participating in faith communities or independent spiritual practices helps to sustain them. Despite these coping strategies, many Mexican American women eventually find that their situations are untenable, and they are forced to seek help (Divin et al., 2013; Fuchsel et al., 2012; Liendo et al., 2011; Montalvo-Liendo et al., 2009). Often, this occurs when they become concerned about the welfare of their children (Divin et al., 2013; Dovydaitis, 2011; Ingram et al., 2010; Kim et al., 2016; Kyriakakis et al., 2012).

Resolution of IPV

Judicious Disclosure

Mexican American women will disclose abuse to receptive family members who have the potential to help (Belknap & Sayeed, 2003). Families that live far away might be limited to providing emotional support; however, those that live close by often provide refuge, money, food, and/or clothing (Kyriakakis, 2014). When family members are not available, Mexican American women turn to women friends. Trusted friends serve as role models, and they provide the encouragement and support that is needed to help them resolve IPV (Belknap & Sayeed, 2003; Kyriakakis, 2014; Liendo et al., 2011; Montalvo-Liendo et al., 2009).

When Mexican American women begin to disclose to others, they might merely seek validation that their situations are intolerable and that there is hope for improvement. Later, they are likely to ask for advice about what to do (Montalvo-Liendo et al., 2009). The latter can lead to calling the police, obtaining protection orders, and filing for child support (Ingram et al., 2010; Kyriakakis, 2014). Initial inquiries, however, rarely lead directly to the resolution of IPV. Instead, intimate partners are likely to repeatedly convince women to retract allegations and return home (Fuchsel et al., 2012; Montalvo-Liendo et al., 2009).

Awareness/Availability of Qualified Help

To encourage Mexican American women to pursue assistance, they need to be aware that confidential and non-punitive immigration, legal/criminal justice, and social services are available. They also need to know that authorities will work within the law to identify the best possible option for them (Ingram et al., 2010). To this end, radio and television broadcasts are recommended to inform women about services that are available. In addition, similar information should be made available at churches, clinics, hospitals, WIC offices, grocery stores, English classes, and child welfare programs such as Head Start (Adames & Campbell, 2005; Ingram et al., 2010; Moya et al., 2014).

There is strong evidence that service providers must be well educated and trained to effectively help Mexican American women resolve IPV (Adames & Campbell, 2005; Belknap & Sayeed, 2003; Ingram et al., 2010; Kelly et al., 2007; Mattson & Ruiz, 2005; Montalvo-Liendo et al., 2009; Moya et al., 2014). For example, first responders must be skilled at making referrals to immigration and legal services. In turn, personnel at these agencies must fully understand and execute the rules and regulations that govern immigration and domestic violence so that Mexican American women are able to safely separate from their abusers, independently navigate through the legal and immigration systems, and move forward with their lives (Ingram et al., 2010).

Along with legal and immigration assistance, social service providers are encouraged to offer women information about financial help, employment opportunities, and supportive services for their children. At all points along the way, providers are urged to demonstrate support, act promptly, and offer clear explanations so that stress can be minimized and women can make timely well-informed decisions (Ingram et al., 2010).

Health-care professionals are urged to inquire about IPV when suspicious health problems or injuries are evident. Owing to the fact that Mexican American women might have limited access to health care, providers are encouraged to tactfully ask about IPV when women accompany their children to clinics. Regardless of the setting, Mexican American women indicate that they are open to questions about IPV, and they are most likely to disclose information when health-care providers are perceived to be sincere, compassionate, empathetic, and trustworthy (Belknap & Sayeed, 2003; Ingram et al., 2010; Montalvo-Liendo et al., 2009).

Initially, health-care providers are encouraged to ask broad questions such as: How are things? Is something wrong? In addition, providers are urged to inquire multiple times and to listen carefully, because trust between victims of IPV and health-care providers could take time to develop (Belknap & Sayeed, 2003; Montalvo-Liendo et al., 2009). Once trust is established, women tend to find therapy helpful, particularly if therapists address traumatic events that have occurred throughout their lives (Dovydaitis, 2011).

Self-Transformation

Once Mexican American survivors of abuse are safe and stable, they tend to invest in themselves by getting an education, improving their language skills, finding employment, and developing relationships with new partners (Dovydaitis, 2011; Kim et al., 2016). In addition, they find it gratifying and empowering to share information about preventing and resolving IPV within their communities (Kelly et al., 2007; Mattson & Ruiz, 2005).

Overall, Mexican American women who overcome IPV perceive that they have been offered positive opportunities to improve their lives (Kim et al., 2016). They are able to financially support themselves and their children, and they have a sense of self-esteem and dignity. They see themselves as transformed, and they are able to fulfill their potential and contribute to society. If they desire, Mexican American women are free to return to family and friends in Mexico (Ingram et al., 2010).

Discussion

Findings from this investigation are largely consistent with those relating to IPV across other cultures (e.g., African Americans, Native Americans, South Asians [Finfgeld-Connett, 2015a, 2015b; Finfgeld-Connett & Johnson, 2013]). Similarities include a history of childhood abuse, patriarchal norms, isolation, lack of awareness of helping services, and distrust of providers (Cummings et al., 2013; Finfgeld-Connett, 2015a, 2015b; Finfgeld-Connett & Johnson, 2013; Klevens, 2007; O'Neal & Beckman, 2016; Rizo & Macy, 2011). Among these, the latter two seem particularly amenable to correction by nurses.

First, nurses are encouraged to circulate information about IPV in clinics and hospitals and at child welfare programs that are frequented by Mexican American women (Adames & Campbell, 2005; Ingram et al., 2010; Moya et al., 2014). Second, to help establish trust, nurses are urged to smile and be pleasant, friendly, and outgoing. They are also encouraged to view each patient as unique and to communicate in Spanish when English poses a barrier (Jones, 2015). Third, when reasonable explanations for suspicious injuries or symptoms are not immediately forthcoming, nurses are urged to sensitively inquire about IPV a number of times (Belknap & Sayeed, 2003; Montalvo-Liendo et al., 2009).

Another way that nurses can enhance trust is by following through with requests in a timely manner (Jones, 2015). To this end, abused Mexican American women recommend allocating money to increase prevention and treatment services (Moya et al., 2014). They also recommend increasing the number of agencies and personnel to expedite the immigration process and to maximize their timely access to work and education (Ingram et al., 2010).

Research

Despite calls to differentiate IPV and its resolution based on culture, it appears that fundamental aspects of this phenomenon are consistent across groups. Currently, a number of rigorous qualitative systematic reviews of IPV across cultures exist (e.g., Finfgeld-Connett, 2015a, 2015b; Finfgeld-Connett & Johnson, 2013), and a rigorous comparison of these findings is recommended to determine if there are any substantive differences.

Limitations

Only 14 unique samples were used to conduct the 19 investigations that were included in this review. Although shared samples across study reports could threaten the generalizability of the findings from this qualitative systematic review, this threat is tempered by the fact that the primary samples consisted of no less than 196 unique respondents who were recruited from across four distinct regions of the United States.

Acculturation was not a focus of the studies that made up the sample for this investigation; thus, the potential impact of this factor on the findings is unknown. That said, nurses are reminded that generalizable research findings do not take the place of assiduous assessment at the time of service, and interventions should be adapted when necessary.

Conclusion

IPV among Mexican Americans tends to be a pernicious problem that is grounded in cultural mores. Barriers to resolving IPV among this group are challenging; however, there are effective ways to reach out. These include circulating information within Mexican American communities about IPV and the help that is available. Strategies for reaching out also include tactfully approaching the topic and building trust-based relationships with patients who present with suspicious injuries or symptoms.

Note

1 Finfgeld-Connett, Deborah, "Intimate Partner Violence and Its Resolution among Mexican Americans," *Issues in Mental Health Nursing* 38(6), 2007, pp. 464–472. Taylor & Francis, reprinted by permission of the publisher (Taylor & Francis Ltd, www.tandfonline.com).

References

Adames, S. B., & Campbell, R. (2005). Immigrant Latinas' conceptualizations of intimate partner violence. *Violence Against Women, 11,* 1341–1364. doi: 10.1177/107780120 5280191

Alvarez, C. P., & Fedock, G. (2016). Addressing intimate partner violence for Latina women: A call for research. *Trauma, Violence, & Abuse.* Advance online publication. doi: 10.1177/1524838016669508

Alvarez, C. P., Davidson, P. M., Fleming, C., & Glass, N. E. (2016). Elements of effective interventions for addressing intimate partner violence in Latina women: A systematic review. *PLoS One, 11,* e0160518. doi: 10.1371/journal.pone.0160518

Belknap, R. A., & Sayeed, P. (2003). Te contaria mi vida: I would tell you my life, if only you would ask. *Health Care for Women International, 24,* 723–737. doi: 10.1080/07399330 390227454

Birks, M., Chapman, Y., & Francis, K. (2008). Memoing in qualitative research: Probing data and processes. *Journal of Research in Nursing, 13,* 68–75. doi: 10.1177/1744987 107081254

Cummings, A. M., Gonzalez-Guarda, R. M., & Sandoval, M. F. (2013). Intimate partner violence among Hispanics: A review of the literature. *Journal of Family Violence, 28,* 153–171. doi: 10.1007/s10896-012-9478-5

Davila, Y. R., & Brackley, M. H. (1999). Mexican and Mexican American women in a battered women's shelter: Barriers to condom negotiation for HIV/AIDS prevention. *Issues in Mental Health Nursing, 20,* 333–355. doi: 10.1080/016128499248529

Divin, C., Volker, D. L., & Harrison, T. (2013). Intimate partner violence in Mexican-American women with disabilities: A secondary data analysis of cross-language research. *Advances in Nursing Science, 36,* 243–257. doi: 10.1097/ANS.0b013e31829edcdb

Dovydaitis, T. (2011). *Somos hermanas del mismo dolor (We are sisters of the same pain): Intimate partner sexual violence narratives among Mexican immigrant women in Philadelphia.* (Dissertation). Philadelphia, PA: The University of Pennsylvania.

Finfgeld-Connett, D. (2010). Generalizability and transferability of meta-synthesis research findings. *Journal of Advanced Nursing, 66,* 246–254. doi: 10.1111/j.1365-2648. 2009.05250.x

Finfgeld-Connett, D. (2014). Use of content analysis to conduct knowledge-building and theory-generating qualitative systematic reviews. *Qualitative Research, 14,* 341–352. doi: 10.1177/1468794113481790

Finfgeld-Connett, D. (2015a). Intimate partner violence and its resolution among African American women. *Global Qualitative Nursing Research, 2,* 1–8. Retrieved from http://gqn.sagepub.com/cgi/reprint/2/0/2333393614565182.pdf?ijkey=nm4isekj7vXn0Kd&keytype=finite. doi: 10.1177/2333393614565182

Finfgeld-Connett, D. (2015b). Qualitative systematic review of intimate partner violence among Native Americans. *Issues in Mental Health Nursing, 36,* 754–760. doi: 10.3109/01612840.2015.1047072

Finfgeld-Connett, D., & Johnson, E. D. (2013). Abused South Asian women in western-ized countries and their experiences seeking help. *Issues in Mental Health Nursing, 34*, 863–873. doi: 10.3109/01612840.2013.833318

Fuchsel, C. L. M. (2012). The Catholic Church as a support for immigrant Mexican women living with domestic violence. *Social Work & Christianity, 39*, 66–87.

Fuchsel, C. L. M. (2013). Familism, sexual abuse, and domestic violence among immigrant Mexican women. *Affilia: Journal of Women & Social Work, 28*, 379–390. doi: 10.1177/0886109913503265

Fuchsel, C. L. M., Murphy, S. B., & Dufresne, R. (2012). Domestic violence, culture, and relationship dynamics among immigrant Mexican women. *Affilia: Journal of Women & Social Work, 27*, 263–274. doi: 10.1177/0886109912452403

Gonçalves, M., & Matos, M. (2016). Prevalence of violence against immigrant women: A systematic review of the literature. *Journal of Family Violence, 31*, 697–710. doi: 10.1007/s10896-016-9820-4

Grzywacz, J. G., Rao, P., Gentry, A., Marín, A., & Arcury, T. A. (2009). Acculturation and conflict in Mexican immigrants' intimate partnerships: The role of women's labor force participation. *Violence Against Women, 15*, 1194–1212. doi: 10.1177/1077801209345144

Ingram, M., McClelland, D. J., Martin, J., Caballero, M. F., Mayorga, M. T., & Gillespie, K. (2010). Experiences of immigrant women who self-petition under the Violence Against Women Act. *Violence Against Women, 16*, 858–880. doi: 10.1177/107780 1210376889

Jones, S. M. (2015). Making me feel comfortable: Developing trust in the nurse for Mexican Americans. *Western Journal of Nursing Research, 37*, 1423–1440. doi: 10.1177/0193945914541519

Kelly, P., Lesser, J., Peralez-Dieckmann, E., & Castilla, M. (2007). Community-based violence awareness. *Issues in Mental Health Nursing, 28*, 241–253. doi: 10.1080/01612840601172577

Kim, T., Draucker, C. B., Bradway, C., Grisso, J. A., & Sommers, M. S. (2016). Somos hermanas del mismo dolor (We are sisters of the same pain): Intimate partner sexual violence narratives among Mexican immigrant women in the United States. *Violence Against Women.* Advance online publication. doi: 10.1177/1077801216646224

Klevens, J. (2007). An overview of intimate partner violence among Latinos. *Violence Against Women, 13*, 111–122.

Kyriakakis, S. (2014). Mexican immigrant women reaching out: The role of informal networks in the process of seeking help for intimate partner violence. *Violence Against Women, 20*, 1097–1116. doi: 10.1177/1077801214549640

Kyriakakis, S., Dawson, B. A., & Edmond, T. (2012). Mexican immigrant survivors of intimate partner abuse: Conceptualization and descriptions of abuse. *Violence and Victims, 27*, 548–562.

Liendo, N. M., Wardell, D. W., Engebretson, J., & Reininger, B. M. (2011). Victimization and revictimization among women of Mexican descent. *Journal of Obstetric, Gynecologic, & Neonatal Nursing (JOGNN), 40*, 206–214. doi: 10.1111/j.1552-6909.2011.01230.x

Mattson, S., & Ruiz, E. (2005). Intimate partner violence in the Latino community and its effect on children. *Health Care for Women International, 26*, 523–529. doi: 10.1080/07399330590962627

Montalvo-Liendo, N. (2009). Cross-cultural factors in disclosure of intimate partner violence: An integrated review. *Journal of Advanced Nursing, 65*, 20–34. doi: 10.1111/j.1365-2648.2008.04850.x

Montalvo-Liendo, N., Wardell, D. W., Engebretson, J., & Reininger, B. M. (2009). Factors influencing disclosure of abuse by women of Mexican descent. *Journal of Nursing Scholarship, 41,* 359–367. doi: 10.1111/j.1547-5069.2009.01304.x

Moya, E. M., Chávez-Baray, S., & Martinez, O. (2014). Intimate partner violence and sexual health: Voices and images of Latina immigrant survivors in Southwestern United States. *Health Promotion Practice, 15,* 881–893. doi: 10.1177/1524839914532651

O'Neal, E. N., & Beckman, L. O. (2016). Intersections of race, ethnicity, and gender: Reframing knowledge surrounding barriers to social services among Latina intimate partner violence victims. *Violence Against Women.* Advance online publication. doi: 10.1177/1077801216646223

Ortiz, V., & Telles, E. (2012). Racial identity and racial treatment of Mexican Americans. *Race and Social Problems, 4.* doi: 10.1007/s12552-012-9064-8

Rizo, C. F., & Macy, R. J. (2011). Help seeking and barriers of Hispanic partner violence survivors: A systematic review of the literature. *Aggression and Violent Behavior, 16,* 250–264. doi: 10.1016/j.avb.2011.03.004

Sabina, C., Cuevas, C. A., & Zadnik, E. (2015). Intimate partner violence among Latino women: Rates and cultural correlates. *Journal of Family Violence, 30,* 35–47. doi: 10.1007/s10896-014-9652-z

Salcido, O., & Adelman, M. (2004). "He has me tied with the blessed and damned papers": Undocumented-immigrant battered women in Phoenix, Arizona. *Human Organization, 63,* 162–172. doi: 10.17730/humo.63.2.v5w7812lpxextpbw

Sandelowski, M., & Barroso, J. (2002). Reading qualitative studies. *International Journal of Qualitative Methods, 1,* 74–108. Retrieved from https//ejournals.library.ualberta.ca/index.php/IJQM/article/download/465/3764

Thorne, S. (2009). The role of qualitative research within an evidence-based context: Can meta-synthesis be the answer? *International Journal of Nursing Studies, 46,* 569–575. doi: 10.1016/j.ijnurstu.2008.05.001

United States Census Bureau. (2011). *Census briefs: Overview of race and Hispanic origin: 2010.* Retrieved from www.census.gov/prod/cen2010/briefs/c2010br-02.pdf

United States Census Bureau. (2015). *American community survey B03001 1-year estimates Hispanic or Latino origin by specific origin.* Retrieved from http://factfinder.census.gov/faces/tableservices/jsf/pages/productview.xhtml?pid=ACS_15_1YR_B03001&prodType=table

APPENDIX 5

Critical Appraisal Skills Programme (CASP) ©

Qualitative Research Checklist 31.05.13

Three broad issues need to be considered when appraising the report of a qualitative research:

- Are the results of the review valid?
- What are the results?
- Will the results help locally?

The following ten questions are designed to help you think about these issues systematically.

The first two questions are screening questions and can be answered quickly. If the answer to both is "yes," it is worth proceeding with the remaining questions.

There is some degree of overlap between the questions. You are asked to record a "yes," "no," or "can't tell" to most of the questions. A number of prompts are given after each question. These are designed to remind you why the question is important. Record the rationale for your answers in the spaces provided.

Screening Questions	*Rationale*
1. Was there a clear statement of the aims of the research? Consider: • What was the goal of the research? • Why was it thought important? • Its relevance	Yes Can't Tell No

(*Continued*)

(Continued)

Screening Questions			Rationale

2. Is a qualitative methodology appropriate?   Yes   Can't Tell   No
   Consider:
   • If the research seeks to interpret or illuminate the actions and/or subjective experiences of research participants
   • Is qualitative research the right methodology for addressing the research goal?

Is it worth continuing?   Yes   No

Detailed Questions

3. Was the research design appropriate to address the   Yes   Can't Tell   No
   aims of the research?
   Consider:
   • If the researchers justified the research design (e.g. did they discuss how they decided which method to use?)

4. Was the recruitment strategy appropriate to the aims   Yes   Can't Tell   No
   of the research?
   Consider:
   • If the researchers explained how the participants were selected
   • If they explained why the participants they selected were the most appropriate to provide access to the type of knowledge sought by the study
   • If there are any discussions around recruitment (e.g. why some people chose not to take part)

5. Were the data collected in a way that addressed the   Yes   Can't Tell   No
   research issue?
   Consider:
   • If the setting for data collection was justified
   • If it is clear how data were collected (e.g. focus group, semi-structured interview, etc.)
   • If the researchers justified the methods chosen
   • If the researchers made the methods explicit (e.g. for interview method, is there an indication of how interviews were conducted, or did they use a topic guide)?
   • If methods were modified during the study. If so, did the researchers explained how and why?
   • If the form of data is clear (e.g. tape recordings, video material, notes, etc.)
   • If the researchers discussed saturation of data

6. Has the relationship between researcher and   Yes   Can't Tell   No
   participants been adequately considered?
   Consider:
   • If the researchers critically examined their own role, potential bias, and influence during:
     • Formulation of the research questions
     • Data collection, including sample recruitment and choice of location
     • How the researchers responded to events during the study and whether they considered the implications of any changes in the research design

Screening Questions	*Rationale*

7. Have ethical issues been taken into consideration? Yes Can't Tell No
Consider:
- If there are sufficient details of how the research was explained to participants for the reader to assess whether ethical standards were maintained
- If the researchers discussed issues raised by the study (e.g. issues around informed consent, confidentiality, or how they handled the effects of the study on the participants during and after the study)
- If approval was sought from the ethics committee

8. Was the data analysis sufficiently rigorous? Yes Can't Tell No
Consider:
- If there is an in-depth description of the analysis process
- If thematic analysis is used. If so, is it clear how the categories/themes were derived from the data?
- Whether the researchers explain how the data presented were selected from the original sample to demonstrate the analysis process
- If sufficient data are presented to support the findings
- To what extent contradictory data are taken into account
- Whether the researchers critically examined their own role, potential bias, and influence during analysis and selection of data for presentation

9. Is there a clear statement of findings? Yes Can't Tell No
Consider:
- If the findings are explicit
- If there is adequate discussion of the evidence both for and against the researchers' arguments
- If the researchers discussed the credibility of their findings (e.g. triangulation, respondent validation, more than one analyst)
- If the findings are discussed in relation to the original research question

10. How valuable is the research?
Consider:
- If the researchers discuss the contribution the study makes to existing knowledge or understanding (e.g. do they consider the findings in relation to current practice or policy or relevant research-based literature?)
- If they identify new areas where research is necessary
- If the researchers discuss whether or how the findings can be transferred to other populations or other ways the research may be used

INDEX

Page numbers in italic indicate figures and in bold indicate tables on the corresponding page.

Lightning Source UK Ltd.
Milton Keynes UK
UKHW020906080421
381413UK00020B/843